IVAN SPENCER

"...the trees of the field
shall clap their hands together"
in worship of God
their Creator.

Now, there are the sturdy oaks,
the stately elms,
the giant mahoganies,
the prim cedars—
and the swaying willows.

Flexible beyond all others,
the willow responds to air currents
with utter freedom;
to sway gently in the slightest breeze,
or to toss crazily
in gale winds.

But respond it must,
for it is created dependent upon its environment
of wind...and water.

So was Ivan Spencer,
and the "Elim" that he founded.

# IVAN SPENCER
## Willow In The Wind

by

Marion Meloon

Logos International
Plainfield, New Jersey

*Thus saith the Lord that made thee and formed thee...Fear not...For I will pour water upon him that is thirsty, and floods upon the dry ground: I will pour my Spirit upon thy seed, and my blessing upon thine offspring: And they shall spring up as among the grass, as willows by the watercourses.  Isa. 44:2-4*

Willows mark out the location of the watercourses for the thirsty traveler through an arid land. Their roots mass about the river bed and draw moisture long after all else is dry.

The willow's usefulness lies in its *flexibility*. Its branches respond to the slightest movement of wind and water currents.

The word "willow" means "intertwining." Willows are interrelated in nature and grow in thickets that form about water. They are linked with their habitat.

# CONTENTS

# FOREWORD

A lovely portrait of my father hangs on the wall of the main lounge at Elim. I pass through the lounge several times each day. Every time my father's eyes follow me across the room—it almost seems that "he being dead" yet seeth! The gleam in his eyes and the marks on his face call to mind some of God's disciplines in his life as well as some of the "wood-shed" disciplines in mine.

A son of the soil and of frugality he remained through his more than 80 years a farmer at heart, planting seeds in God's good earth and in the hearts of young men, and nourishing the tender plants which sprang up. Many of the scripture lessons he taught were illustrated from farm life. Though he sought to implant in all eight of us children the same appreciation for agriculture, none of us could match his pace in the field nor in the milking stable. Much of his day by day inspiration and guidance for life's challenges came out of communion with the Lord early in the day at the farm, or in later years in his garden and orchard.

The church of the 20th century is deeply indebted to these pioneer trailblazers who followed their Grail with zeal and abandon. Though often misunderstood they were individuals consumed with a vision from God and a purpose to see its fulfillment. So it was with my father who—with *revival* emblazoned on his mind and heart—gave himself to see revival in the broader sense in his day.

Open fellowship, appetite for revival worldwide, a "hands off" approach to worship and spiritual ministry, priority on gifts of the Spirit and holiness which led to deeper teaching on relationship to Christ, continual questing for God's best, and an aversion to human organization: these are some of the emphases for which he stood. Through my life I have faced inward conflicts over some of these but have come to both appreciate and identify with them, though at times my father doubted the purposefulness of my goals.

The lives of my wife and myself have been closely interwoven with my parents. To my mother's life of dedication, I am also indebted. Her personality and ministries, though opposite to dad's, had a great part in molding my life, and the spiritual and practical life of the school.

Much more than a half century of exposure to such a man as my father, to his life and his vision, reveal both the weaknesses and the strengths of his personality and as well his capacities for and in God. My years in childhood and youth, and later when seeking to help hold up his hands as a partner in the work, were a great learning experience. It was impossible to be near him without being deeply affected by his humble yet purposed sincerity. Many times have I thanked my God for the privileged heritage I have enjoyed.

When Elim's leadership fell my lot and I discovered more of my own inadequacies—I longed for "Dad" to be close by (and was grateful when he was near enough so I could call on him). When his promotion from this life came I was suddenly overwhelmed by the fact that in truth I now belonged to the elder generation—and could no longer look to him and his contemporaries for guidance. The beloved cognomen "Dad Spencer" as used by hundreds says more than any further commendation I could give.

Our author, Marion Meloon, in the years she has been a part of Elim's staff has become as one of our family. Her patient and persistent research in archives covering the past eighty-five years, and her consistent quest for accurate detail from all of us reflected her genuine motivation for the past twelve months. She committed herself to present dad's life story in such a way that we, who are enjoying the benefits of another insweep of heavenly tides, might benefit from the lessons learned.

Thanks, Marion! Beautifully done! And from the life described herein, may God's glory and design be seen— though set forth in an earthen vessel of another generation.

"For Thine is the kingdom and the power and the glory, forever. Amen!"

Carlton Spencer

# AUTHOR'S NOTE

I suppose what really interested me in this writing assignment was my own experience with Elim over the years. I was not always an insider. From my remote and comfortable position with another fellowship I often shared in the criticisms leveled at Elim. But age and experience have a way of mellowing opinions and broadening perspective, and I began to value Elim's open fellowship and freedom in worship.

Though Southern Baptist in background, I came into the Pentecostal experience early in life and soon enrolled in a small Pentecostal Bible school in New Hampshire. I remained to teach and there experienced the joys of Holy Ghost visitation. I drank deeply of the refreshing Latter Rain revival, also getting acquainted with Elim, a sister school then located in Hornell, N.Y.

After teaching for fifteen years in Northwood Bible School, and then in New England Bible Institute, I turned to pioneer church work in northern New England. From more than ten years of this isolation, secular exposure and ministry in a limited fellowship, I was drawn to reenter the Bible School cloister. But Elim was not a cloister—not really. Its global vision, in action, gave me windows on the world that stirred an almost forgotten hunger. And the ease with which they worshipped challenged my New England reserve. Adjustment was traumatic, but I was convinced that these distinctives were worth the risk.

Nor can one be a part of Elim for eight years without sharing the founder's passion for revival—a sweeping visitation of the Spirit that alone can meet humanity's need. (It is in this broad sense of the word "revival" that I have chosen to write this story.)

As the reader peruses this account of a revivalist's life, he may feel the same vacillation of faith and despair that I sensed upon writing it, but I pray that the residue shall be a refined faith in the purposes of God to "pour out of His Spirit upon all flesh." My motive for writing has been to glorify God—the God of the prophet Joel, and of Ivan, and of today's Church.

Assisting me in this task of much research, reminiscence and prayer, in writing and rewriting, were the Elim president and school family, the Spencer family and friends, former Elim students and staff, and not a few typists. To all I owe a great debt of gratitude, but especially to Carlton and Elizabeth for their loving, wholehearted cooperation, even when reminiscence became painful. I ached with them as I probed for answers that might bless the reader.

Above all else that I have learned from this story is the truth that "When I am weak, then am I strong."

# STATEMENT of RESEARCH

The author relied on two major sources of information: printed matter, drawn mainly from Elim's archives, and interviews with family, friends, and former students and staff members—often taped for accuracy. As for research via publications, the following are the chief sources: *Chronicles of the Faith Life* by Mrs. E.V. Baker (now out of print); volumes of the monthly *Trust* magazine, dating from 1913 and published by the Elim Faith Home and Rochester Bible Training School; volumes of the monthly *Elim Pentecostal Herald* magazine, published by the Elim Bible School of Ivan Q. Spencer — dating from 1931 and extending over a thirty-year period; numerous newspaper clippings preserved by friends and relatives; school annuals, catalogs, etc.

Some information stemmed from the author's own observations and experiences with Elim, intermittently, over a period of thirty years.

For the sake of realism and readability the author exercised the privilege of reconstructing scenes and conversations, in keeping with known facts and fragments of actual conversations. The truth of Ivan Spencer's story, often "stranger than fiction," is ample proof of its relevancy and value. This is the reason for writing this story—. "Now all these things happened unto them for examples, and they are written for our admonition, upon whom the ends of the world are come." (I Cor. 10:11)

# 1

*The Beginnings Of A Man Of God*

Ivan Spencer was born in 1888 of sturdy homesteaders in the Allegheny foothills of northern Pennsylvania. When his parents, Merritt and Alice Spencer, were married, they received as a wedding gift from Merritt's parents a 160-acre tract of virgin forestland. Its steep hillsides, gouged by a cascading stream which divided the land two ways, delighted the beauty-loving Alice and challenged the muscular manhood of slim, moustached Merritt.

The ring of axe on wood, the crash of falling timber, the rasp of the saw, and pounding of the hammer brought into existence the first humble home of the young couple. Facing the creek and barely higher than its waters at floodstage, the two-room dwelling with loft overhead housed the Merritt Spencer family for ten years—much longer than they had intended. The barn stood across the creek from the house on the part of their land that adjoined his parents' farm. To connect barn and house, Merritt had built a simple bridge of rocks across the creek that was inundated each spring by capricious floodwaters. Above the house and barn, on each side of the creek, lay the more level land for farming and pasture.

"We'll plant corn on this side," Merritt had said to Alice with a proud sweep of his hand. "Then, over there, will be oats and winter wheat. . . . " Thus they planned, and worked, and the farm expanded.

What a proud day it was when their first baby arrived—a son. They named him Vern. Alice's lovely face glowed with motherhood, and Merritt touched the tiny fingers and said, "He'll be a big help on the farm."

When their second son, Ivan, was born, Merritt's work-worn face relaxed in a smile, and he declared to Alice, busily bathing the tiny body, "I'll make a farmer out of him—a good one—and our farm will be the best around."

In rapid succession, the family came—two daughters, Blennie and Emma, then last, another son, Leslie.

Life for Merritt had become one round of rigorous winters and toilsome summers. The fun-filled hours of the first months of marriage had given way to the mature responsibilities of making a home for his growing family. The boy became a man in the process, but not happily so. The harsh circumstances of life tinged his voice with sharpness and added austerity to his expression. Alice retained her sunny disposition, but carefully watched his moods and often resorted to her Bible for comfort and strength.

Clearing the forests for planting was a job for a strong man, a stronger ox team—and the boys. When a tree was felled, and the log cut into lumber, the remaining stump with its upturned spread of roots would be pulled to the side to form, with other stumps, fences dividing the fields. Rambling grotesquely across the landscape, these root fences were as beautiful as driftwood, and fitted the rugged hillsides they still adorn. Roots also provided the only fuel for warmth and cooking. They served an even greater purpose one day when little sister Emma was in trouble.

An angry bull, straying from the pen behind the barn, caught sight of her brightly clad figure and charged after her. She ran for the house as fast as her legs could carry her, but the distance between bull and girl was closing faster than that between her and the kitchen door. Feeling the bull almost upon her, Emma stumbled in her panic and rolled—right under a massive clump of roots beside the well. Its sturdy projections held the bull at bay and provided a cage of safety for the frightened child.

After the trees had been cleared, another task remained before plowing could be done. All rocks, from hand-sized stones to giant boulders, had to be removed. Sometimes it seemed there were more rocks than soil. This backbreaking, hand-tearing task was a family project which continued until the plow could safely furrow the land for planting. To Ivan, "the seed which fell upon stony ground" became a remarkably plain text in later years.

In planting time, Ivan pulled heavy branches—the poor farmer's substitute for a harrow—across the oat-sown furrows. In harvest, from the time Ivan was barely big enough to pull his little homemade wagon, "Ike," as his dad called him, followed his father over the rough plowed fields. The father's sweeping cradle-scythe left a glistening swath of felled sheaves, which he tied on his return across the field. Ivan's job was to load the heavy scythe onto his little wagon and tow it back across the rough ground to the beginning of another swath. The performance was repeated again and again throughout the hot August days, and developed in Ivan a capacity for work that undergirded all of his later years.

But childhood was not all backbreaking toil. A pleasurable mixture of fun and creative expression also found its way into their primitive living. There were many adventures with the sled which Ivan ingeniously contrived of wood and metal parts gleaned from barn and farmyard. One wintry day,

Emma accepted his invitation to slide downhill with him, toward the creek. The bridge being out, they would hopefully make the turn before reaching the creek, and their speed should send them upward toward the barn, Ivan thought.

The steep icy decline sent them downward at top speed, snow flying as they veered from side to side. Ivan thrilled at the speed, then quailed with fear as, suddenly, a runner broke through the crust, and the sled turned sharply. In another moment, sled and riders shot into the icy waters of the creek.

Ivan's first words as he staggered dripping to the creekside were, "Emma, don't tell father!" Emma understood. Worse to Ivan than a damaged sled and chilling spill was his father's common expression of stern displeasure, "You stupid fool!"

One day when Ivan was six years old, his father announced that the time had come for their long-awaited permanent home to be built on the bluff above them. Lumber had been piling up for many months, in readiness for the project. Ivan's part would be the busy job of errand boy, with nails, tools, and pieces of lumber twice his size to deliver in unceasing repetition.

His father's ability to erect such a splendid home seemed like magic to Ivan. Eight rooms with woodshed and outhouse, a barn, and a wagon house. The fear he had of his father became muted somewhat with respect and admiration. And surely Merritt must have been proud of his sturdy young sons, growing into the capable farmers that he had dreamed they would be. But already Merritt could sense in Ivan an enigmatic quality that boded ill for his dream. The lad was a bookworm, and though he had dubbed him a "stupid fool" for what he thought were good reasons, it never crushed the boy's enthusiasm for school. Then there was his strange appetite for religion—a reflection of Alice's foolishness, it seemed. And here Merritt was haunted by a memory.

One day he had caught Alice reading the Bible to a fascinated Ivan. Tired and hungry, unreasonably furious, he had torn the book from Alice's hands and thrown it across the room. Long after the echoes of his harsh words died away, the look of her wide, fear-filled eyes and white face had haunted him.

But in spite of these "weaknesses" in Ivan, Merritt recognized in him the makings of a real farmer with a sensitivity for the animals that neither he nor Vern had. Perhaps Ivan's success with the animals lay in his love for them, something more than the usual respect a farmer has for a good workhorse or a cow that exceeds milking expectations. Merritt had learned early that cash income was readily available through taming cheaply bought, unruly horses or training and yoking young oxen and reselling them at a higher price. When farmers came "shopping," it was not the imposing figure of the man that clinched the deal, but the slight figure of the boy who emerged from the barn with the animal, after complying with his father's command, "Ike go in and harness that mare." The boy's magic with unruly animals turned a nice profit, and Merritt could ill afford to lose Ivan to the ethereal realm of scholarship and religion.

When school started each fall, Ivan was up at five in the morning to feed the livestock, milk the cows, and curry the horses. Then he would hurry to the house for a quick breakfast of cornmeal mush and "coffee" made from burnt breadcrumbs, pick up his bucket lunch of fried cornmeal mush patties, and head off for school with his brothers and sisters.

It was a two-mile walk to the Sayles schoolhouse, a one-room wood-frame building with a potbellied stove which never quite adequately heated the high-ceilinged room with its large windows. Absorption with his studies cut Ivan out of the undercurrent of classroom devilry often present, but recess time found him teasing the life out of one and all.

Home again by late afternoon, Ivan would hurry out to the barn for more chores. Then there was always wood to be chopped before returning to the large cheery kitchen for a simple, hearty supper. After the table was cleared, he settled down with his books for brief hours of enthusiastic study.

When Ivan finished his grammar school years at Sayles, his impressive progress made high school advisable. Merritt considered the recommendation uneasily, but finally agreed. He arranged for Ivan's enrollment at the nearest high school, West Burlington. A neighbor offered to let Ivan live in a little house he owned near the school. Vern attended also that first year, and Emma was sent along to keep house for the boys.

In one of Vern's classes, a teacher challenged the students by saying, "If you can save your first hundred dollars, you'll never be broke." Vern took this literally, and through the summer worked hard to earn his first one hundred dollars. After that, he grew scornful of both Ivan and school, and devoted himself fully to moneymaking. This drive for money motivated him throughout his life, and he later became rich enough to place thousands of dollars and government bonds in many banks of the area. Though the time would come when Vern's hoarded monies would serve the Lord, it was not until after a lifetime of miserliness had bound his soul.

It was a Sunday morning, and the Spencer family occupied their usual places in the little West Franklin Methodist church. Ivan sat beside his father in the choir loft. Alice and the rest of the family filled the front pew. The humidity and forced quiet had so enervated the congregation that the minister must have despaired of holding their attention. He could not see the young parishioner in the choir loft who listened intently, his face revealing deep concentration.

Then a stir of air through the church window wafted the smell of new-mown hay to the nose of the elderly minister.

Memories stirred, and didactic tones gave way to nostalgic reminiscence. His text from the Book of Acts became a launching pad for an exploratory trip into the past.

Ivan's gaze was riveted on the old preacher. The text had fired his imagination, and a curious blend of vivid pictures surged through his mind—"cloven tongues like as of fire," "a rushing mighty wind," and a group of Jews all speaking in many strange languages. Then there was Peter, just a poor ignorant fisherman, preaching a sermon that netted the church three thousand souls!

Awe crept into Ivan's heart when the preacher read of the lame man at the beautiful gate of the temple, all twisted and ugly, waiting for God. True, he was asking for money, but surely it was the power of God he wanted. And at Peter's command the man had arisen and gone joyously leaping through the temple. Ivan wondered with amusement what would happen to this sleepy congregation if suddenly he were to leap up in joy. He was just swallowing a chuckle when the minister's voice droned out the declaration, "Of course, such things do not happen today. The early church needed signs and wonders to prove the reality of Christ and the Holy Spirit, and to get the church underway."

Ivan was crestfallen. How tantalizing it all had been. Was there nothing left to religion but this sleepy wordiness? Was this delicious longing all for nothing? The preacher's next words jarred him back to attention.

"However, often on through the centuries there have been times when parts of the Book of Acts have been repeated—" He paused, then a new note of enthusiasm came to his voice. "Why, even in the early days of Methodism, people at times acted just like they did on the Day of Pentecost. I've been told that back before this church was built, there was a circuit-riding preacher who came through this area. He held some meetings and got some people converted—mostly women. After he was gone, the women met for prayer meetings in their homes. They'd get so shoutin' happy that their strange worship got known throughout the area.

"Then one night, a group of young men in the village got together for a good time. After playing a lot of games, one said, 'We've played all the games we know, but we haven't had a Methodist meetin' yet!' As they began to mimic the women, the power of God got ahold of them, and they couldn't stop. One of them managed to get away, and on his way home, he met a sister just returning from her prayer meeting. He told her what was happening, and she got him to take her back to the young men—who were still crying out to God in an agony of conviction. They all got converted that night—in fact, so well converted that they built a church, a Methodist church!"

The preacher's voice had risen with excitement, and the people were listening now, curious. Still unnoticed was the young face in the choir behind the preacher, eyes bright with unshed tears of longing. But Ivan's mother noticed from her place in the front pew—and waited.

Suddenly it seemed to Ivan that a dam let loose inside him. Sobs burst from him that stunned the restless congregation into stillness, and suspended the preacher in mid-sentence. Ivan felt a vicious jab in his side—his father's elbow, no doubt. What humiliation and anger would be his! But there was no stemming this force that poured through him in floods of tears and wracking sobs. He sensed he was but a channel for a Power greater than he, and helplessly gave himself to it.

When the sobs subsided, the minister pronounced the benediction. The congregation, uncomfortable with the unfamiliar, were relieved to get out to their horse-drawn buggies and back to the safety of Sunday dinners and farm chores. Ivan's father escaped to the haven of his carriage, but not without hissing the familiar indictment, "You stupid fool!" The troubled mother shared a few words of concern with the pastor and hustled the other children out the door as the minister turned to Ivan.

Awkwardly, his arm went about the young man's shoulders, his confusion matching Ivan's. He had often sensed in this boy a spiritual questing that was beyond his understanding. Many were the questions Ivan had posed, sparked by discussions in his Sunday school class, that he, the preacher, had only lamely answered. Now he realized he must say something—but what? His words served only to confuse Ivan the more. "Look son, don't take things so seriously. God loves you; you're a good boy. Be content with that."

The ride home was miserable. Vern poked fun. Ivan's father was angry and silent. His mother cast anxious glances his way, while Emma clasped his hand tightly and blinked back sympathetic tears. But deep inside, untouched by the emotional tension about him, Ivan sensed a growing conviction that he had started to find God. What was that verse the pastor had read? "The wind bloweth where it listeth, and thou hearest the sound thereof, but canst not tell whence it cometh, and whither it goeth." That wind of the Holy Spirit had reached him this morning! Perhaps this was the way one got understanding of the Bible, by personal experience with the Holy Spirit. He would start reading about it again this very afternoon. But his dad mustn't catch him at it—or Vern!

# 2

## "As The Twig Is Bent..."

The following summer of 1909, Ivan was sitting out in a field with a neighboring farmer for whom he was temporarily working. They had been picking corn all morning, and the noonday sun shone hotly down upon them as they husked the ears. Sweat ran in muddy rivulets down Ivan's face, and he smeared one across his cheek with an impatient brush of his calloused hand. He felt irritable.

The older man had been talking about the Fairview Methodist Church, which stood on a corner of land behind where they sat on the hillside. As he recounted "the good old days," all the old frustration began to surface in Ivan. He tried to hide it by gazing off across the valley, admiring the growing patchwork pattern of the settlers' fields, and enjoying the occasional cool breeze that fanned his cheek. Memories would come, however—the memory of aspirations born in that little church service in the valley, of the frustrating days that followed when he searched the Bible for new meaning, only to find the veil still there. Now here he was having to listen to all this religious talk from his neighbor just when he was trying to forget it all.

10

Suddenly aware of the farmer's silence, he turned to find his neighbor gazing intently at him. He flushed. Had the farmer guessed his thoughts? Perhaps he had been in that service when Ivan's sobs had broken up the meeting!

With a cautious look, the farmer startled him with a question. "Have you ever been called to preach?"

"No," Ivan answered, aghast at the thought, then curious. "Have you?"

"Yes," was the revealing answer.

"Well, why aren't you about it then?" Ivan asked with the blunt simplicity that characterized him.

The farmer told him the story of his life. He spoke of a "born again" experience, which he had to explain to Ivan; then of his call to preach the Gospel. His words were few and halting, and his troubled gaze sweeping over farm and fields gave wordless interpretation as to what had replaced the call of God in his life.

Finally, changing the subject, the farmer announced, "Guess it's about time for lunch. When you're finished there, come on in." He strode off across the field with his slumped shoulders and arms filled with the produce that occupied his life. Ivan's eyes followed him, trying to understand.

So that was the key to knowing God, he thought—a "born again" experience—born of the Spirit to a new life when you confessed your sin and turned your future over to Christ. Why hadn't he seen it before?

When he responded to the dinner bell, Ivan startled the farmer's wife by asking to see her Bible. This was an embarrassing request, for the wife had to look long to find it, and then had to dust it carefully to hide its disuse.

Leaving the table early, Ivan returned to the hillside where the words "born again" had entered his vocabulary. There he found them again in John 3, along with his verse about the wind blowing where it will. As he read and reread, the hungry spark in his soul flared, then flamed. Casting himself upon the pile of cornhusks, he sobbed out to God his need for forgiveness and rebirth. Then, spent at last, he lay quietly waiting. Softly, peace came. Oh, how clean he felt—and what joy! Quietly, then louder, he worshiped his Lord.

Then God spoke. *Ivan, will you preach for Me?*

Awe and privilege, and hilarious joy, flooded his soul. There was no hesitation.

"Yes, Lord!"

"Son, are you sure that's what you want?"

The words rankled Ivan. He had just confided to his minister that he was "born again," that he at last knew God in the personal way he had been seeking, and that God had called him to preach.

The minister's reaction was so guarded and questioning, Ivan thought. Why wouldn't a minister understand such things?

"Sir, what more could I want from life than to serve God and make Him known to others?" Ivan suddenly felt more spiritual than his pastor and quite capable of showing him—and the world—what a fine minister he could be.

His shoulders squared, he turned to go, then suddenly understood the minister's hesitation. How could he, a poor ignorant farm boy with no money, little education, undersized and by no means handsome, shy, pitifully slow and hesitant in his speech, become a preacher? Turning again, he saw on the pastor's face a pity and an anxiety for his welfare that he had missed before.

"I guess what you mean is that I'm not the preacher-type, and maybe I'm not," said Ivan. "But Peter was only a fisherman, and he became a great preacher after Pentecost. Couldn't the same thing happen to me?"

The minister smiled in encouragement. "Why don't we wait and see? You attend seminary and get some training, and we'll just see."

Ivan's father was not so encouraging. "What a stupid idea!" he roared. "Everyone knows you're a farmer—and a good one, too. Surely the Almighty wouldn't make such a mistake. If you must go to school to prove you're unsuited, go. But not one cent of my money will pay for it."

Again Ivan's anger flared. A father should be proud to have a son in seminary! As for finances, well, God had called him to preach, so God would somehow provide the money. He would prove to his father that seminary was not a stupid idea.

The problem of finances was solved by the pastor's suggestion that he sell books to the other students and pay for his own books and tuition from the profit.

Thus prepared to support himself, Ivan caught a train which took him a hundred miles across the state to the beautiful campus of Wyoming Seminary, located on the Susquehanna River not far from Scranton.

What a strange new world seminary was for him. Only his love for books and desire to preach could have made him stay there, for although he was intelligent, he lacked the sophistication of most of the seminarians, and was keenly aware of his lack of polish in manner and dress. He suffered much from a sense of inferiority even when surrounded by friends who appreciated his easygoing disposition. Perhaps his father had been right about this being a stupid idea. Perhaps he had been wrong about his call to preach.

Ivan's inner turmoil over his awkwardness and the reality of his call was aggravated by philosophical arguments as to the Bible's interpretation. When in a New Testament class his professor had advanced the views of higher criticism, Ivan was nearly undone. He had already come to realize through his experience with his own pastor that not all would understand his spiritual experiences, but here the professor tried to explain his experience away as an emotional trauma. Sick at heart, he read his Bible long hours into the night in an

13

effort to regain the joyous faith that had been his since that day in the cornfield.

Then he became ill, stricken with a fever that seemed to drain his shaky physical and mental reserves. When the days passed and he only grew weaker, he received a summons to the Dean's office.

Standing before the Dean, hands gripping the desk to keep from swaying, he heard what he feared to hear from the first day.

"Mr. Spencer," droned the Dean, "your fever leaves you too weak to continue in classes. The nurse tells me that you may be suffering from typhoid. It would perhaps save the school an epidemic if you were to go home and rest." Then he added, somewhat tenderly, "You could return next term if you are well enough."

"Yes, sir," was the only answer Ivan could summon to his lips. He would return home in failure. His father and Vern, and maybe even his pastor, would say, "I told you so." There would be no preaching for the rest of his life, only farming. Not that he didn't like farming—he could make good at that, too—but what about God's call?

Stumbling out of the office and up to his room, he passed fellow seminarians who gazed after him in pity. "Too bad," he heard one say, "but he didn't fit in here, anyway. He'll never be a preacher."

Anguish tore at his heart as he packed, slipped down to the train station, and departed. Through the night, the train jerked and whistled its laborious way through the mountains while Ivan wept unashamedly. Pain wracked his body with every jerking curve of the rails. His head pounded. The fever had swelled his lips and eyelids and left his face white and drawn. Perspiration, then chills, increased his agony. He remembered that Jesus had healed Peter's mother-in-law of a fever. Couldn't Jesus heal today, heal him? Ivan wanted to believe, but the suave apologies of his professors tormented

14

his thoughts and seemed to barricade even his prayer. "Oh God!" was all he could cry.

*Don't be discouraged, son; I will heal you if you'll trust in Me.* The words spoken deep in his soul were vividly real, and a balm to his crushed spirit. The relief and joy of God's felt presence so relaxed him that he went to sleep.

Hours later, Ivan awakened to find his fever broken and his strength returned. And the revelation of the truth that Jesus heals today so rejuvenated his faith that when he swung off the train at his home station, Ivan knew he had not returned from seminary defeated. His path to preaching might have to take another route than seminary, but he was sure he would make it.

Back on the farm, Ivan accepted the scorn of his father and Vern with a combination of grace and superiority. After all, God had healed him, revealing His power, so Ivan was vindicated. His first Sunday back at church the minister had not said, "I told you so," as he feared, but rather had appeared disappointed. However, when Ivan told him of his experience of divine healing, the minister looked downright displeased.

"If I were you, Ivan, I'd not talk about this to others. You might be misunderstood and be called a fanatic. This could hurt your ministry later on." But Ivan's testimony was not to be stifled. If Jesus healed today, then others should know about it, too. And he never did keep silent on that subject, though he found no one in his church or community who would believe him. His mother's disbelief that his healing was from God disappointed him the most, and Ivan retreated behind the new wall of misunderstanding between them, a wall created by his insistence on a doctrine little understood at that time. The hurt was mutual. Ivan had yet to learn that the truth must be shared in the Spirit of truth, that doctrine—to be palatable—must be seasoned with love. It was not until many years had passed that he again enjoyed full fellowship with his mother.

One day in midsummer Ivan and his two brothers undertook the job of digging a deep ditch behind the barn. Since the labor of digging required no thinking, Vern, the eldest, took the opportunity to question Ivan on spiritual matters. Ivan recognized that the questions were not designed to gain information, but to antagonize and trap him into a fit of temper he'd be sorry for afterward. Ignoring the last question posed him, he directed some questions of his own at Vern, earnestly pleading that Vern get serious with God.

"What do you mean, 'serious'?" Vern fended mischievously. "I *am* serious!"

"Then why don't you give your life to God and let Him change you?"

"P'raps I'm not predestined to," Vern growled, repeating a word he'd heard in last Sunday's sermon.

"That's crazy," Ivan declared, nettled to have theology thrown at him by his godless brother. "Anyone who wants to come to God can. Anyway, you can't use that for an excuse. I've found God, and you can, too!"

Vern grew very angry. Tossing the dirt from his shovel, he turned to Ivan and insisted, "Well, that's the difference between you and me. You are predestined to go to heaven, and I am predestined to go to hell!"

A stunned silence fell upon the three boys. The digging continued without further conversation, each preoccupied with his own thoughts. Ivan regretted that he'd pushed Vern to such a declaration, and Vern felt uncomfortable that he had said such a thing of himself. But young Leslie was the most deeply affected. Vern's declaration made him realize the awfulness of going one's own way without God. He, too, must come to God or join Vern and others on their hell-bound way. Later, in the quiet of his own room, he made a commitment to Jesus Christ that was to lead him eventually into an alliance with Ivan's ministry.

Not long after this quarrel, Vern and Ivan were sent out with their rifles to replenish the family meat supply. After hours of fruitless search, they emerged from the woods onto a neighbor's field where the man was working with his plow. Looking them over, the farmer challenged them: "So you're hunting out-of-season, huh? Well, I'll just tell the authorities about that!" He slid off his plowseat and headed in a hurry for his house.

The boys looked at each other in consternation. A lifelong habit, at the command of their father, had not seemed wrong until now.

"Let's quit," Ivan said, sensing a guilt he didn't like to admit. Together, they headed for home, dreading the interview with their father. Upon arrival, they found him pacing the kitchen, an angry scowl darkening his face.

"Don't you know enough to stay in the woods when you're hunting?" the father exploded in an illogical display of anger.

"Then you heard?" asked Vern, and added, "What can we do?"

Merritt cursed the neighbor, the laws, and the coveted deer. Quieting finally, he moodily announced that he had no money for fines. "Well," he said at last, "I see nothing else to do but to send you boys up into New York State. You can stay with Elwin in Elmira until the matter blows over." Uncle Elwin was his brother and the boys' favorite uncle, though they saw little of him.

An hour later they set out, leaving a sad household. Emma clung to Ivan, sobbing, and mother kissed him goodbye as though he were never coming back, and that troubled him.

# 3

## The Willow Finds Its Watercourse

Life in Elmira was vastly different from life on the farm. There was work, but in the machine shop with Uncle Elwin. The words "stupid fool" seemed never to have entered Uncle Elwin's vocabulary. In fact, he made Ivan feel important and did not laugh when Ivan discussed with him his call to preach. Aunt Lizzie was even more interested in his spiritual welfare, and between the two of them, they managed to rebuild Ivan's confidence in himself and God.

He regularly attended a church where the Gospel was preached, and found fresh inspiration in the services and in the fellowship of new friends.

Word came at last that the boys could return home, but Ivan stayed on in Elmira. The time for his break with home ties had come, and he set his heart to go on with God to the next step.

As spring approached, Elwin sensed a growing restlessness in Ivan. One day he put his finger on the trouble. They were on their way to work, and a balmy spring breeze chased the litter before them down the sidewalk. Uncle Elwin remarked casually, "Beautiful day—almost planting time, wouldn't you say?" Tears sprang to Ivan's eyes as he agreed, then added, "Uncle Elwin, do you suppose I could get a job on a farm somewhere?"

Elwin's hand squeezed Ivan's shoulder. "Been missing it, son, haven't you? Well, I'd say it would be a lucky farmer that would get you. We'll have to look into it."

"Of course I'd only want to go for a short while. I've got to preach, you know. But this machine shop job isn't getting me any closer to preaching, and I was farming when God spoke to me before. I just feel like maybe that's where I should be until the way opens up for preaching."

"Sure now, I can understand that," Elwin agreed, wondering at the persistence of this young man in something so unlikely.

Arrangements were made with a farmer near Macedon, on the outskirts of Rochester, New York, and Ivan settled into a new venture that was surely a further step in God's will.

One night after the chores were finished and the family had gathered around the table for their evening meal, the conversation swung to religion. Ivan was glad for the opportunity to share his limited knowledge of the Bible with his new friends. As he talked, he was conscious that the farmer's wife understood and shared his excitement over the things of God. She broke in finally to tell him that she knew God was real because He had healed her of a serious illness.

Ivan was elated. He plied her with questions: "How did it happen? Did God speak to you? Have you told others? What did they think? Do you know anyone else who believes this way?"

On the last question, she told him of services at a place called Elim Tabernacle in Rochester, where she had been prayed for and was healed. Ivan found a ready listener to his own story of healing, ending with, "and God has called me to preach."

A silence fell upon them. The farmer who'd done more

listening than talking spoke. "I'd say if you're called to preach, you shouldn't be trying to farm. Isn't there a seminary you can attend where you can get your training? How about the Genesee Wesleyan Seminary at Lima only 'bout fifteen miles from here?"

Ivan's heart sank. Was there no other way? Seminary to him meant only a bottleneck for his spiritual progress—how could he face it again? If only he could find a school that shared his experience and could lead him on into the "more" of God that he sensed there was for him.

Then the wife's excited voice broke in. "There's a Bible training school connected with the Elim Tabernacle that trains ministers and missionaries. It's small, and only a two-year course, but perhaps that is where you should go. Why don't you come to church with us Sunday and see about it?"

Only one service was needed to convince Ivan that he had found his spiritual home. The Rochester Elim work, once called "the powerhouse of the east" and later known as "Old Elim," had been founded in 1895 by the Duncan sisters, who were Rochester residents and daughters of a retired Methodist minister. Both father and daughters had suffered much for their convictions regarding divine healing and the availability of God's supernatural power for the whole of the Church age. Ostracized from their mother denomination, they had expended their spiritual fervor in establishing the Elim Faith Home on East Avenue in Rochester, engaging, in the meantime, in mission work among the down-and-outers. The Home became a spiritual center for many who were dissatisfied with nominal Christianity. The mission, in which they were assisted by their godly father, flourished, and notable conversions took place. There they learned many lessons in the life of faith, fitting them for the further ministry God had for them.

When evacuation of the mission became necessary, they purchased the block where their Faith Home and Print Shop were located, and built the Elim Tabernacle, adjoined by a large educational unit. The oldest sister, Mrs. E.V. Baker, shouldered the bulk of the responsibility for administration of this multiple ministry. Her experience of divine healing, her call to preach, and her intense pursuit of spiritual truth made her the unquestioned leader of the group.

In 1906, God led them to start a training school for young people whose hearts were stirred as theirs for revival to come to the Church. It was about the same time that young Ivan in the little West Franklin church was strangely moved to weeping and great hunger, longing for the days of power known by the early Church; and closely timed as well with the Azusa Street, Los Angeles, visitation, which was the birth of the Pentecostal movement.

In 1907, Elim experienced its Pentecost. Mrs. Baker relates it thus in her *Chronicles of the Faith Life:*

In our June Convention were two brothers who had received this experience, and we asked them to present the subject. . . . Almost the entire convention attendance became seekers at once. . . . The power of God was manifested in a manner almost indescribable. . . . Many were prostrated under the hand of God, speaking in tongues, singing and prophesying. . . . Truly the "latter rain" had come, and God was doing a new thing in the earth. . . . We had heard about the "heavenly choir" . . . we actually heard its notes sounding out like a great oratorio of angelic voices. . . God anointed some with no natural power of song . . . heavenly music like waves of the sea for power, and again soft and sweet as the cooing of doves.

A professor of music was present, and his report of the event was also printed:

To my amazement and admiration they sang so

perfectly, so harmoniously, so artistically as no trained choir could sing. Their intonation was sure, with no deviation of pitch. . . . Every singer was given up to God, guided by the Spirit. To me as a musician, this singing is conclusive proof of the absolutely divine origin of this present manifestation of the Holy Ghost.

Into such a rich spiritual heritage Ivan stepped that first Sunday of attendance at the Elim Tabernacle. Being a shy and reserved person, he was somewhat frightened by the joyful praises and outward manifestations of God's presence, but he recognized immediately his spiritual kinship with these people. He set himself in alignment with all that came forth, both in the preaching of the Word and in the ministering of the gifts of the Spirit, and like a sponge, he thirstily drank in the great spiritual principles of the faith life, of divine healing, the Baptism in the Holy Spirit, the second coming of Christ, and sanctification by substitution—"Christ in you the hope of glory."

When fall came in 1911, Ivan enrolled as a student in Elim's Rochester Bible Training School, along with other young men and women of similar experience and calling.

Three conventions were held annually at the Elim Tabernacle, and the Rochester Bible Training School students benefited from the ministries of many great spiritual leaders who stirred the hearts of students like Ivan Spencer to missionary fervor.*

*Convention speakers during Ivan's school terms and following included: A.G. Ward, father to "Revivaltime's" C.M. Ward; J. Roswell Flower, who became a foremost leader in the Assemblies of God; A.S. Booth-Clibborn of England; Elizabeth Sisson and D.W. Kerr, both nationally known Bible teachers; and such missionary statesmen as William F.P. Burton of Africa and Noel Perkin, then of South America and for many years Missionary Secretary of the Assemblies of God. From Elim's staff, besides the rich ministries of Mrs. E.V. Baker, Susan and Hattie Duncan, came the developing teaching ministry of John Wright Follette, an RBTS graduate of 1911, destined to become an internationally known Bible teacher. Later there was Gustave Schmidt, an RBTS graduate of 1917, founder of that great missionary organization that has changed the face of Christian

To Ivan, that first convention was unforgettable. People streamed into the tabernacle, many from great distances, and packed out the building to the doors. The platform was filled with ministers and missionaries, some of them former students. And how that congregation sang! Then the missionary candidates shared brief and fiery exhortations, followed by an outpouring of intercession for them by the congregation. At the climax, all surged forward to present their offerings in a spirit of hilarious giving, leaving the offering baskets overflowing for missions.

Ivan was astounded at the obvious unity among the ministers, who represented a variety of denominations. New to Ivan also was the emphasis upon an endtime revival, a great revival that would precede the tribulation and Christ's return, "this revival coming through the present Pentecostal movement."

The altar service found Ivan among the seekers, though his wonderment at others' responses to the Spirit interfered with his own. He watched and prayed, catching a bit of reflected glory as the blessing fell on others. Some would break out in ecstatic language or song, or would be slain in the Spirit, falling backward onto the floor. One of the students began to laugh hilariously, even reeling to and fro, drunk in the Spirit. Ivan noticed that this student retained his blessing long after the service was over. In fact, the next day, his face shone so that he was hardly recognizable. Ivan hungered to be similarly God-possessed.

Nor was this amazing power present only in services. More

Mission in Europe—"The Russian and Eastern European Mission," later known as "Eastern European Mission." It was Gustave Schmidt who referred to "Elim" as "the spiritual slaughterhouse . . . for here the old flesh is being worked on from a hundred different angles. I discovered (as a student) that I was a great chunk of 'flesh' clothed with selfish plans and desires. After a great struggle, I threw up my hands in complete surrender. . . . He has called me to Russia." Present students of today's "Elim" can appreciate this sentiment expressed by an earlier student in training.

Other missionary speakers, many RBTS graduates, were William and John Norton of India; Ralph Riggs of Africa, later a leader in the Assemblies of God; Alfred and Joseph than once the Spirit came upon them as they were gathered in the dining room to eat. The blessing on the food would extend into a full-blown praise service in which all took part. Once during conversation at the table, one of the students became so literally drunk with new wine that she could not sit up and had to be assisted from the dining room. A guest seated nearby remarked, "I've heard of those at society banquets falling under the influence of liquor; but to be taken drunken out of a Pentecostal dining room is certainly a new thing!"

Ivan also noted that divine healing was not only preached, but demonstrated, again and again. This was not new for him, but there was a detailed teaching on Christ's coming that strangely intrigued him: many raptures, the varied participants in each, the chronological order of such events, all became the thrust of some of the convention messages.*

To Ivan at this time, in spite of what may have been unnecessary complications (which were compounded in his own ministry later), the precious naked truth of Christ's personal return, to receive to Himself "a glorious church without spot or wrinkle," fired his soul with spiritual vision, and new love for the Lord.

Though Ivan did not receive his personal Pentecost until his second year, he nevertheless delighted in these manifestations of the Holy Spirit. His reserved nature kept him from freedom of expression in the services, but he did experience many "overwhelmings of divine love" like those of evangelist Charles Finney, whose ministry shook Rochester in earlier days.

But something else stirred in Ivan Spencer besides spiritual

Blakeney of India and Africa; Charles Personeus of Alaska; Yumna Malik of Syria; Anna Ziese of China, and many others—seed-planters for today reapers!

*A 1918 *Trust* magazine carried an article worth repeating in this connection. Entitled "The Peril of Overthinking," it stated:

Sometimes we spoil by subtle analysis some truth which would be much better received by just taking it into our hearts as it comes to us, and acting upon it as swiftly and joyously as we can. Instead we imagine that by probing a matter relentlessly we shall be breezes that first year in Bible school.

It was a wintry evening, after a long full day of classes. The bell announced supper, and Ivan joined the other students as they filed into the dining room. He soon was aware of guests being seated at the table of a certain young teacher named Percy Back, an Englishman who had graduated from Elim two years before. Ivan was always painfully aware of his irritating country ways when he was in the presence of the prim and proper Percy, but tonight, the young lady next to Percy attracted his attention. She was a stranger to Ivan, but not to his dreams. Every inch a lady, as Percy was every inch a gentleman, she nevertheless appealed to Ivan as his ideal—in poise to offset his awkwardness, and in vivacity to overrule his shyness.

Ivan pretended to eat as he feasted his eyes upon her trim though plain appearance, the thick silky coils of her hair, and her winsome expression. The other young female students paled in her presence. "Just girls yet," Ivan thought, as he compared their gay banter with the poised and pleasant manner of this guest.

Supper was over and the guests gone before Ivan learned that the admirable young woman was Percy Back's sister, recently arrived from England, and obviously from another culture than his. But he didn't forget her, he couldn't.

surer of it, and so we find one great truth after another losing its luster. It was meant to help, and instead it has become just one burdensome problem more; and still the victim of overthought will go on trying to cure his malady by more of the vice that produced it.

# 4

*A Woman Of God In The Making*

Annie Minnie Back was born in January, 1891, in Salford, Lancashire, England. She was the last child of a mother who had borne nine children previously, all of them boys!

The small cottage of Worthy and Ann Elizabeth Back was not a wealthy one. Nor was it an altogether happy home. But the thin wail of the newborn daughter came as a welcome sound to the ears of the waiting family. The two small sons, Edwin ("Ted") and Percy, when admitted to the forbidden nursery, peered curiously into the cradle, their faces lighting up with wonder and awe. Mother Ann's worn face softened with gladness over this bright female spot in her life, but Worthy's good spirits more probably came from his bottle than from the new little bundle of life who now shared their cottage.

Who can tell the thoughts of that mother-heart as she cradled her namesake to her bosom, and dreamed her dreams? Certainly this new Annie must be spared the tragic marriage that had blighted, and ended, her own happy girlhood. And this wee one's choice of a husband must be wiser than her own second choice had been, for liquor must not cast its ugly shadow over this sweet pink face in her arms.

Clinging desperately to the fragment of hope her Anglican Church offered, Ann would bundle her little daughter in warm blankets, dress up her fine little sons as best she could, and set off for the worship service each Sunday morning. There, the rich liturgy would soothe life's hurts, and she would return to her dreary home with such phrases as— "The Lord is my light and my salvation, whom shall I fear; the Lord is the strength of my life, of whom shall I be afraid;" "I had fainted unless I had believed to see the goodness of the Lord in the land of the living;" "Many are the afflictions of the righteous, but the Lord delivereth him out of them all"—to hold her steady for another week.

The children were still small when Worthy's occupation as a carpenter took him to Northfleet, a suburb of Gravesend, downstream from London on the Thames River. Annie's growing up years were spent here in a little rowhouse, one of a row of identical homes, with a door and one window front and back, no more than 15 feet wide, and sharing its side walls with its neighbors. A tiny fireplace in each room offered the little heat that kept life in the body throughout blustery winter months.

Here the Anglican Church School enrolled Annie Minnie Back into its curriculum which included many hours of Bible teaching and memorization. Her keen mind absorbed its beautiful expressions readily, and as she developed mentally, she also grew into a winsome lass, well-adjusted socially and content with life as it came. Her mother's sacrifices to groom her child well, paid off in Minnie's happy acceptance at school and church.

When spring came, Annie Minnie would join her brothers in excited exploration far beyond the confines of narrow city streets. How delightful were the waving grasses and rippling marsh waters, the salty warm breezes and sunshine pouring down over all. Her naturally sunny disposition expanded under the influence of a happy school and church life, the close friendship of brother Percy, the loving watchfulness of her mother, and Worthy's proud boastings, "She's my daughter!" to his drinking mates.

When playing hard one day, Percy fell and suffered a slight concussion. To help the already overburdened mother, the vicar of their church took Percy into his home for his convalescence. He kept him until he finished his schooling that year, then found a job for him in a hotel in London. It was here in London that Percy attended a Brethren hall and gained a personal experience with Christ. His conversion was outstanding and his spiritual appetite was whetted for even more than the Brethren offered.

He returned home, worked for a while with his brother Ted, and diffused the warmth of his spiritual experience throughout his family. But though they were impressed, they were not converted at that time.

Then a shadow fell over their home when mother Ann contracted tuberculosis, and daughter Annie Minnie bore more and more of the home responsibilities. Gradually health's bloom faded, as coughing spasms weakened the once sturdy mother. Minnie's lot was to empty sputum vessels, a repulsive task for the daughter who had been taught to love the fine and beautiful in life! These coughing spells also worked a hardship on Worthy, whose smoking often triggered them. He gave up the habit with anxious willingness, however, and a monstrous guilt.

Ted, now married and the father of one child with another on the way, decided to better his family's chances in life with a try for better employment in the new world of Canada. Percy agreed to go with him. It was a sad Minnie who saw them off on the ship and returned to the dreary life of caring for an invalid mother.

Minnie's schooling came to an end in her fourteenth year,

after the family moved to Birkenhead, where Worthy worked on the Liverpool to Manchester canal. To Worthy, fettered by drink, the fading away of his sweet little wife was only one more indictment against his guilty soul. He idolized his lovely, faithful daughter, but hated himself for the poverty that necessitated her leaving school.

In the providence of God, Percy heard of Elim while in Toronto. The two brothers moved soon after to Rochester, New York, Ted making a home there for his family who joined him. Percy enrolled as a student in the Rochester Bible Training School. Here his spiritual fervor, his fine tenor voice, manly appearance, and his English poise with clipped accents made him a favorite immediately. But he didn't forget his family. He often sent choice devotional books and letters to his invalid mother, to encourage her faith.

"So mother, you see there is a real experience of salvation for you," wrote Percy in one letter. "You don't have to 'hope' you are saved, you can know it, because His word says, 'He that believeth on the Son *hath* everlasting life . . . *is passed* from death unto life.' It's so real! Then He wants to fill you with His Holy Spirit. How you need this Comforter, mother, and He is yours for the asking—' The Father will give the Holy Spirit to them that ask Him.' And oh, how He wants to heal you—I'm sure He *can*, for I see many healings taking place here. You and father and sister must come to America, just as soon as you are able."

To the mother, whose weakness and paroxysms of coughing now confined her to her bed and denied her the solace of Sunday morning worship, the words came as glimmering rays of hope on a black landscape.

But one day the frail mother slipped out of her hard earthly life, and Minnie clung sobbing to her breathless body.

"We will go to America, child," Worthy said, as he clumsily tried to comfort his girl-woman daughter. It was the least he could do for her, after all she had suffered from his wrongdoings. In time, they set sail from England—the seriously eager young woman and the father with sagging shoulders, pain-darkened eyes, and unsure steps. It was to Ted's home that they came to live.

On a hot day in July, 1909, just two years prior to Ivan Spencer's enrollment at Elim, Minnie Back attended her first service in the Elim Tabernacle, on her first Sunday in America.

She sat proudly beside her brother Percy, now a teacher in the school, conscious of admiring glances in her direction. The meeting was about to begin, and already she sensed the difference from her Anglican background.

The gracious Mrs. Baker opened the service with a call to worship that brought a response amazing to the young English lady. True, Percy's letters had warned her of "joyful praises" and a "liberty in the Spirit," but her reserved nature was hardly prepared for the volume of praise that ascended from every throat but her own. Even Percy seemed part of it as he joined his fine tenor voice in the strangely blending harmonies of the congregation.

Minnie felt like an outsider, and her happy excitement faded into confusion as the service progressed. That their joy was real, she could not doubt, and she observed wistfully the peaceful, happy faces about her. She was relieved when Mrs. Baker announced her text and plunged into the message of the morning. Her fears faded as strange new truth fed the fires of spiritual hunger.

" 'Quench not the Spirit,' intimates that someone had been doing so," began Mrs. Baker. "Here Paul is saying to such, 'Quit trying to put out the fire of God in your lives.' There are those today who maintain that the least emotion manifested openly is a mark of human weakness or soulish activity. . . . When a fire is burning clear and bright, there is movement and crackling noise; but when a fire is quenched, there is smoke; and a murky atmosphere is the result."

Minnie felt rebuked for her criticism of their emotionalism. What did she personally know about a "fire" anyway, she thought. Mrs. Baker continued:

"What gain is there in the Pentecostal experience? It is a matter of cooperation with God in His dispensational movements. The danger among believers in our time is that of being satisfied with a past experience of holiness and failing to see the day of His visitation in the present manifestation. . . . The great mistake of those who oppose is that of attempting to analyze every operation of the Spirit and formulating a doctrine where no doctrine is intended. It has been well said, 'You should take up truths as flowers are gathered in gardens, because of their beauty and desirability: not made more beautiful or desirable from a knowledge of their scientific names or of their exact place in the vegetable kingdom.'

"The question is simply this," Mrs. Baker concluded. "Is this thing called 'Pentecost' from God? If so, I am bound to commit myself to it, even though I am unable to harmonize or analyze all that I find. . . . Doubtless Satan has tried to imitate, as did the magicians in Egypt, but it has only proved the presence and mighty working of the Holy Spirit which like Moses' rod, will sooner or later swallow up the rods of the magicians. . . . The 'latter rain' promised by Joel is undoubtedly falling, and if some hailstones from the enemy seem to be intermingled, 'He who hath begun a good work will finish it'—and therefore will we not fear! If the demonstrations of the Spirit were safe for Christians in the first century, they are safe for Christians of the twentieth."

The words had fallen strangely on Minnie's unawakened heart, but as she left the tabernacle that morning on her brother's arm, she was sure of one thing. These people had a reality she did not have, but she wanted it. In the succeeding services, her confusion and sense of spiritual estrangement deepened, but so did her hunger for God.

31

Some weeks later, Percy invited Minnie to dinner with him at the school. When she arrived, she was delighted to find another guest present, a Miss Lawson who had once visited their home in England. It was soon obvious to Minnie that Percy had arranged the meeting for her spiritual welfare. But though she longed for help, Minnie shied away from spiritual discussions. The afternoon sped by, and the young ladies decided to continue their acquaintance in a trip to Highland Park that evening.

When they boarded the trolley an hour later, the sky looked stormy, and alighting at the park entrance, they felt the first drops of rain. Dashing for the bandstand on the hilltop, they stumbled up the steps, breathless and laughing, just as rain poured in thunderous orchestration on the bandstand roof.

Conversation was impossible, so the girls sat and watched the drama of the storm-lashed gardens. To Minnie, the storm seemed a fitting symbol of her spiritual confusion. Strange that they should come to the park on such an evening as this, she thought. Usually the park was crowded, but tonight they were alone, and forced to sit and think. She sensed the Divine Arranger in the circumstance, and as the rain abated, she glanced uncomfortably toward her companion. Miss Lawson quietly asked, "Why are you not happy? You aren't, I can tell."

Such adept directness stripped away Minnie's reserve, and she poured out her confusions, fears, and longings. Miss Lawson listened, then placed her skilled finger on the source of confusion as she asked, "Perhaps you are not yet 'born again,' and this is why you feel like an 'outsider,' as you put it. You may know Christ as an historical figure, but not as your personal Savior and Friend, as the Lord of your life. Is that the way it is?"

Sobbing, Minnie agreed. "But how can I know Him like that?" she wailed. "I always thought I was good. I've been very religious. But now I can see that isn't what being a Christian really is. How do I get in?"

Quickly, Miss Lawson assured her that Christ forgives and receives all sinners, the wicked and the religious, and that He would give her the new birth to bring her into the new life that she craved. Two heads bowed in earnest prayer, and time blended with eternity for a few sacred moments.

Later, when the rain ceased and the setting sun slanted golden rays through the bandstand, the young ladies made their way back down the hill to the trolley with hearts rejoicing.

Percy left that year to pastor in New England, and a year later, Worthy Back moved to Macedon, taking his daughter with him. Here Minnie attended the Baptist church, and her father worked on the barge canal. That was the year also that a farmer near Macedon hired a young farmhand from Elmira—Ivan Spencer. But in God's unfathomable economy, Ivan had sought fellowship at Elim Tabernacle, rather than the Macedon Baptist Church.

It was also God who led Ivan to enroll that fall of 1911 in the Rochester Bible Training School, just when Percy Back returned to RBTS to serve again on the staff, as teacher and dean of men.

During that school year, Ivan was sent to the Macedon Baptist Church to speak in a service. That week, a friend burst into Minnie's room with the excited announcement, "A young man from RBTS is speaking in the service Sunday—we can't miss it!" But miss it Minnie did, and ironically because of a visit from Percy. When later Minnie visited and had supper at the school, she did not notice the young man who admired her from a distance.

The following summer, Ivan returned home to help his father and Vern on the farm, while Minnie returned to Rochester and to the Elim Tabernacle.

This time, the English transplant took root in Pentecostal

soil and drank thirstily of the spiritual fountains of truth. How she yearned for that new dimension of the Spirit that comes with the Baptism in the Spirit, but her reserved, fearful nature held her bound—until the night God caught her off guard.

Her father was attending the service, and she sat beside him, aching over his strangeness to the new life that was hers. As the meeting progressed, she empathized with him in his confusion and lack of understanding of such worship. When the altar call was given, she slanted a look his way, questioning him with her eyes for his response. He only shook his head and looked miserable. She ran to the altar, fell upon her knees, and cried out to God for her father's salvation, completely forgetful of herself. And the Spirit moved in, first in deep intercession, then in joyous singing in another language. It was glorious, for not only had she been filled with the Spirit, but she was sure that all would be well with her father's soul.

From that night on, Worthy began to change. His drinking ceased entirely, and he enjoyed his attendance at the Tabernacle. And from that night until now Minnie's chief ministry has been in intercessory prayer and worship.

When school began in the fall, the church took on new life from the fresh input of the students. Since Minnie and her friend Margaret Mosher were the only young people of the church, they gladly welcomed this youthful influx. But due to a lack of finances, Ivan was not among the returning students.

One Sunday evening later that fall, Minnie arrived at the Elim Tabernacle late for service. She slipped into a seat reserved for her in the back by Margaret. A few minutes later, the door behind them opened to admit another latecomer. He seated himself in a back pew on the other side, directly across from her. Slight, a pleasant round face, she observed, and countrified in manner and appearance. But she felt drawn to him and knew immediately that he was special to her.

"Who is he?" she whispered, prodding Margaret.

"Oh, him? He's a last-year student, Ivan Spencer. Must have just returned late."

Ivan had not noticed his "ideal" seated across the aisle, nor the sensation he was creating in that young lady's heart. He entered into the worship with quiet abandon, determined that his senior year would be a life-changing one. A long hard summer, the death of his grandfather, and his financial frustrations had ripened his hunger to the point of desperation. He must receive the Holy Spirit's fullness, he determined, and he must find out God's will for his life. Intently, he listened to Mrs. Baker's challenge, so suited to his need.

"God is disciplining you into a pliability that will not question Him, but will do what He asks you to do, and will do it instantly. I remember when the Lord put us into this Elim Home, a $35,000 property with only $3,500 in hand towards it. I said, 'Lord, I cannot do it,' and the Lord said, 'Child, I could have had every dollar here this morning to pay for that property, but the way I am going to take is for your blessing.' And that way was to move in under that tremendous load, and have a lot of Christian friends say, 'It is wrong to be in debt, and therefore you are all out of God's order,' but we knew God had spoken. Oh, the volume we could write over the steps God has taken us, the pliability He was working in us, and the faith!"

As her message continued, Ivan's roots went down into fresh truth that would one day undergird similar moments of financial pressure and misunderstanding in his later life.

When the service concluded, Ivan was surrounded by welcoming students. It was not until the greetings were over that he noticed the two young ladies waiting to greet him at the door. Immediately he recognized *her*. As their eyes met, he was aware that she shared his feeling. He accepted Margaret's introduction calmly, but from then on, he addressed the young ladies as "Margaret" and "Miss Back."

Percy soon became aware of his sister's attachment to Ivan. Making his deanly roomcheck one day, he found Minnie's picture occupying a place of prominence on Ivan's dresser. Irritated, he snatched it up, then replaced it facing the wall, and walked out in cold silence. Ivan's anger flared, and the distance between them became a battleground.

Later, to Minnie, Percy remonstrated, "That country bumpkin! He'll never be a preacher!" He proceeded to arrange for visits and parties that would make Minnie known to other more suitable young men. But Minnie continued to gravitate toward the student whose twinkle and illuminating smile did things to her heart.

Ivan vacillated between ecstasy over Minnie's attentions and agony over Percy's scorn. Only his preoccupation with spiritual pursuits, with many hours spent upon his knees, held him steady during those days.

As convention time drew near, Ivan's desperation reached its peak. Spiritual highlights of the convention precipitated the crisis for him. In the first service, from where Ivan sat with the students, the platform presented an imposing array of guest ministers, among them Percy Back, soloist for the convention. Ivan fought resentment, then anger and humiliation, as Percy introduced his song with perfect ministerial dignity. He cut a striking figure, Ivan noted furiously, as he poured forth in rich tenor tones a spiritual challenge that brought the congregation to its feet in praise and worship. That is, all but Ivan, who sat as if glued to his seat, and burned in anger. Only when Mrs. Baker arose to minister did he arouse from his bitter thoughts. Hungrily, his spirit reached out for "meat in due season."

"God knows the weak places in every soul and knows just what to do to bring us out of our narrow selves into His abundant life. . . . In no other way will the flesh die more quickly than when one steps out to trust the Lord fully on all lines."

That "flesh" was his problem, Ivan could now clearly see. *Pride*, not the pride of appearance, talent and poise such as Percy might justifiably possess, but that pride of life, ego, that stung from the very lack of these. Ivan's moment of truth had arrived, and he humbly listened as Mrs. Baker continued.

"Once when thinking over the question of death to self, I asked the Lord to show me the quickest and most effective way to bring the self-life to death. I knew that judicially we had been crucified with Christ, but now to make it practical in daily life. He said to me, 'If you will *praise Me* for everything that I allow to come to you, self must die!' I could see that this would keep one in the will of God."

Ivan felt his soul stripped by the Word, and felt sure that everybody saw his guilt and conviction. As a matter of fact, one did. And when Ivan ventured a look in her direction—he always knew where she sat in a service—their eyes met. His pleaded, hers smiled encouragement, and Ivan turned with relief to listen to the next speaker, a sprightly lady in her seventies. Elizabeth Sisson was nationally famed as a Bible teacher, and her words to Ivan's ears were as fire touched to tinder.

"We should all be ready and open to the voice of the Spirit for any fresh word He may have to say to us. . . . Keep 'under the water wheel,' near to God, where the flow of the Spirit is fresh and constant. . . . Move out of any stale Pentecostal experience into the freshness of God's present working in and through the heart and life.

"To those seeking the Baptism, our attitude is now, not of waiting and praying and seeking God, but rather that of 'receiving'; as He breathes out, we can breathe in, and thus we may be filled. . . . There must be a coming *in* His saints before there can be a coming *for* His saints."

A burst of praise followed her stimulating remarks, and Ivan was excited—it was like opening the door to a treasure room. He responded with others to the altar call.

Facing up to his "flesh" had brought him to that point of desperation that releases faith. As is often the case, the quietest soul when invaded by the Third Person of the Trinity may become the noisiest. With such reservoirs of the hot lava of truth building up within, there could not fail to be such an eruption of worship when the release came as to completely overflow the boundaries of religious propriety. Praises poured forth from his lips in heavenly language with gushings of holy laughter. Like the lame man at the gate of the temple, he went leaping and praising God until restraining hands overcame his exuberance.

Something happened to Ivan Spencer that night that no one present could doubt.

# 5

*Revival Firebrand Flames And Dims*

To Ivan Spencer, the Comforter had come as dynamite, toppling hangups of the old life and providing vistas of conquest that put his soul on tiptoe after God. It was therefore unlikely that he would sit through the upcoming missionary convention untouched.

Perhaps it was the challenging message from India's missionary Albert Norton that stirred his response to world need; or it may simply have been the white heat fervency of his spirit making him a ready listener to the voice of God. Whatever triggered the event, it was at this time in Ivan's life that he felt a call to India's needy millions; and from this time until he set foot on India's soil, the vision remained with him.

Admittedly, there is a glamor to overseas ministry that can intrude itself into the pure motivation of any youthful enthusiast. Quite possibly, Ivan's call also suffered from this very human tendency. But God help the Church when its youthful dreamers, endowed with the physical strength and lofty idealism that the job demands, sit at home awaiting the perfection of their motivation. Ivan by now had become painfully aware of his earthiness—and the shocking revelation would continue in days to come—but the "Treasure" in his "earthen vessel" was his delight, and to share his blessing seemed an imperative. God's hand was on Ivan, relentlessly, and his response was a model of instant, wholehearted obedience.

In the fresh glow of his Baptism in the Spirit, each day became an adventure of release for this otherwise reserved young man. When a class began with worship, Ivan joined the praising lustily, and chapel services often caused him to act like a calf loosed from the stall. The lame man at the gate had nothing on Ivan. Gale winds had blown upon this willow—small wonder that it tossed so wildly. But when again and again the school leaders felt it necessary to squelch his fervor, his reaction was hurt and indignation that they could be so lacking in spiritual understanding.

Some time later, impatient to begin his ministry, and confusing passionate zeal for spiritual preparedness, Ivan made a decision that could have been ruinous. Seeking out his principal, Mrs. Baker, he asked permission to leave school to go out into an evangelistic ministry. His reasoning was simple.

"God has now filled me with His Spirit and given me a great desire to see souls saved. I am only wasting my time staying here when I could be out preaching the Gospel."

Though Mrs. Baker understood his zeal, she was also aware of his immature judgment and natural inabilities. She had heard one of the teachers, after a homiletics class, remark, "That Ivan Spencer will never make a preacher!" She knew from a long life of experience that God did not always overrule in a dramatic way one's lack of eloquence. She also knew that natural eloquence was not an essential in the ministry, but that an established faith, a disciplined spirit, and a mature viewpoint were. Her wise answer was doubtless a pattern for his own to his students in days to come.

"Ivan, though your personal Pentecost is a powerful

factor—an even more enabling force than you now realize—your future ministry to be most effective must flow from a disciplined, matured character. There is a purpose in the length of our course here at Elim, and development of character is part of that purpose. Stay on, and let God deepen the channel through which the Holy Spirit can flow in a deeper way."

So Ivan continued as a student of RBTS, and of the school of God built into its curriculum.

The Duncan sisters were strong in their emphasis on holiness—the crucifixion of the old life with its works of the flesh, and the replacing of self by Himself through the sanctifying process of daily dying to self, in all its insidious forms.

As is often the case with an enlightened conscience, Ivan's conception of holiness became a preoccupation with his unholiness. How he wept as he sensed for the first time the unholiness of natural ambition, and of his resentments and animosity toward those who would hinder him in his ambitions—his father, Percy, his teachers.

One day as he sought God, more in despair than faith, he suddenly envisioned the Lord, resplendent in white flowing robes. Jesus seemed to be looking at someone and beckoning, "Come!" Then Ivan saw a little urchin, a dirty rascal of a fellow, who started to run happily toward the Lord, then hung back and looked down at his dirty clothes. Again "Come!"—and again he started to run toward Jesus. After several such hesitations, he ran into Jesus' outstretched arms, and immediately, he was enfolded in an embrace that hid him behind the white flowing sleeves of the robe.

Ivan stood wondering at the audacity of the dirty little fellow, and amazed that Jesus would risk embracing him, when suddenly the urchin's head bobbed up from behind Jesus' arms and looked square at Ivan. Ivan blinked in amazement—the little fellow's face was his!

The tremendous truth of Jesus' love for him in all his dirtiness—the flowing whiteness mercifully hiding his shame—broke upon Ivan as a new revelation of God's love. Not only did Jesus accept him, but He covered his unholiness with the beauty of His own holiness. Ivan rose from his knees and went back to his studies with a balanced perception of sanctification—and a new love for Jesus.

Another time, at the close of a difficult day of classes, Ivan wearily climbed the stairs to the prayer room, which had become more familiar to him than any other place. Here moments seemed like hours, or hours like moments, depending upon His presence. Tonight, Ivan sensed God's presence from the moment his knees touched the floor. He raised his hands in jubilant praise, laughing, then weeping in the Spirit, as he abandoned himself to know God's purposes for his life.

Slowly his surroundings receded, and he became conscious that the Spirit was etching pictures upon his mind—revelatory pictures which he sensed to be the Pentecostal movement in days to come.

He saw groups and handfuls of Spirit-filled believers scattered throughout the world. God showed him that the purpose of this worldwide diffusion was to "bear the light of the supernatural ministries that He had given them to the people of their localities, and to intercede for greater things for them." Next, he saw the movement grow in numbers, while manifestations of supernatural power decreased. Then there came a sifting and testing time. God promised, "But in that day, I will take My people, discipline them, and use them." This was followed by an awareness of a glorious outpouring of the Holy Spirit.

Suddenly Ivan was confronted with large flaming red letters spelling "REVIVAL." He jumped to his feet, blinking and rubbing his eyes, but wherever he looked that day—and for days after—the flaming word was there, promising, challenging, proving that he had met with God. He had been called to revival ministry, and he knew it. He left the prayer room in the certainty of divine commission.

Even Percy had to concede that God's hand was upon Ivan Spencer for ministry. Just how this untalented but deeply spiritual young man would fit into the ministry, he could not guess, but the Spirit's anointing for service was obvious.

With the lifting of Percy's disapproval, and the jelling of his call to the ministry, Ivan was ready to give attention again to his courtship of Minnie. That her father would approve seemed certain, and he lost no time. Seeing her home after church on the trolley became a regular gallantry, with ulterior motives. There was always the visit in the kitchen afterward, over cream puffs—which Ivan later declared Minnie had used to bait him.

One evening, Ivan appeared at the kitchen door of the Culver Road home where Minnie and her father lived and worked as housekeeper and gardener. She had entertained him here before—he was a favorite with the family who employed her. But tonight was different, and though the cream puffs were as delicious as ever, and the kitchen setting no different than on other visits, yet this night was marked. And they both knew it.

Over the months of courtship, Ivan's shyness had evaporated, but tonight it returned full force. Minnie's ready laugh was nervous, then silent. Suddenly Ivan blurted, "Will you marry me?"

It was the age-old question, needing no garnishing, and requiring as direct an answer.

"Yes," Minnie promptly replied, and the shyness of the moment was smothered in the warm first embrace that followed. Then came a torrent of planning, late into the night.

On April 30, 1913, in the parlor of the bridesmaid's house,

a residence located on the Elim property, a young man and woman exchanged vows whose echoes never died away. A jubilant group of students formed most of the small congregation, but there were also the Duncan sisters, present to extend their blessings, and some Elim guests, including Ivan's admired missionary friends, Dr. and Mrs. A.L. Slocum on furlough from India. Minnie was simply gowned and wore Mrs. Slocum's bridal veil. The officiating clergyman filled in as soloist as well, and performed both tasks with perfect poise and a clipped English accent.

Elim's *Trust* magazine for the month of May carried this announcement:

### Wedding Bells

We have the pleasure of announcing another student wedding, that of MISS A. MINNIE BACK to MR. IVAN Q. SPENCER (Class of 1913), on the eve of April 30.

Mr. and Mrs. Spencer will reside in Spencerport, near Rochester, where they will be pleased to receive a visit from all old students. In the name of R.B.T.S. and Elim Home, we extend most hearty congratulations, and a wish for days of happiness, till the Lord comes.

Both of these dear young people are fully consecrated to God and under the Pentecostal baptism of the Spirit, and we trust for much precious service for the Master.

To Ivan, life on the farm with Minnie was the icing on the cake. Love burst into full bloom, and his pride was undiluted when they attended the community church that first Sunday and Ivan introduced "my wife, Mrs. Spencer."

He delighted in the pretty blush that would follow such proud moments, and he loved to tease his city-girl wife as he introduced her to farm life and American homemaking.

In his past months of absorption with school and prayer and courting, Ivan had almost forgotten how nice the hay smelled, the delight of the animals nuzzling his hand for feed, the rewarding buckets of warm, foaming milk, and all the other barn sights and sounds. At times his introduction of the livestock to Minnie brought frightened screams, and a clinging that he took advantage of for an extra kiss.

As they became better known in the community, Ivan was asked to preach on occasion at the community church. These were proud but anxious times for Minnie, who desired that her husband would be accepted.

With the progression of the summer, Ivan kept long hours out in the fields under the hot sun. Minnie broke the hours of separation by carrying out cool refreshing drinks to the farm laborers, enjoying the attentions of one particular farmhand for a few choice moments.

Summer planting gave way to fall reaping, then the shorter winter days of chores and more leisure hours together. Now they had a secret they shared, and Minnie's hands were usually busy with sewing tiny garments.

More leisure time meant time to think. and Ivan realized, as Minnie already had, that his priorities had slipped. Having no transportation but horse and buggy, they had gone to Elim Tabernacle only a few times during the summer and fall. In his busyness, with no reminder other than Minnie's uneasy concern over their spiritual welfare, Ivan had begun to lose sight of his objectives.

With great remorse, Ivan set himself again to seek the Lord. Over the winter months, the conviction grew in him that to remain in Spencerport, where all was so idyllic for them, would only further sedate his spiritual senses. He must cut away the shorelines and launch out, believing God to open doors of ministry. With a child on the way, Minnie should be near his mother. The next step must be one he'd never choose, left to himself. They must go back to his home, brave his family's "I told you so," please his father by helping him on his farm, and await God's opening into some ministry.

Reluctantly, he faced Minnie over the breakfast table with the account of his convictions. Minnie heard him out placidly, then declared, "Ivan, I've felt the same way for months—it's what I want, too." Grabbing her up for a hug and kiss, Ivan gaily announced, "Then back home we go—all three of us!"

Vern had by now married and bought the homeplace from his parents. They, in turn, had rented a little house across the ravine. It was to this home with his parents that Ivan and Minnie moved in the summer of 1914, though later Merritt and Alice moved back in with Vern and his wife, Flora. In this little home, in the month of July, Minnie delivered her firstborn, a son—Ivan Carlton.

What excitement invaded the neighborhood upon his arrival! When Ivan appeared at Vern's with the proud announcement, Alice and sisters Blennie and Emma set out on a run, down through the ravine and across the fields, to greet and gingerly touch the tiny first grandchild cradled in Minnie's arms.

The months fled by. Ivan held services in various churches in the area, including his own home church. He even held a week of services in the little school that he attended as a boy, feeling more liberty there to preach the full Gospel than he did in the churches. But there was no attendant stir of the Spirit such as he had witnessed at Elim Tabernacle. He was frustrated trying to preach a message that was neither understood nor accepted.

Pentecostal churches in those days were few, and though Methodist churches spread across the great northeast, few of them were ready to accept a preacher of Pentecostal persuasion. However, when Percy encouraged Ivan to attend the Methodist Conference and accept a pastorate if one were offered, Ivan did go and accepted the pastorate of the Reading Center Methodist Church in the Finger Lakes region of upstate New York.

Settled into a pastorate, Ivan felt he had surely arrived. Life was sweet, with a happy parsonage home, a loving family, a friendly admiring congregation, and a pulpit from which he could preach his heart out—which was just what he did. But as the Sundays passed, his sermons failed to gain the response he longed for. He impatiently blamed the sleepy congregation, then himself—for lack of power. After a typical dispiriting Sunday, Ivan knew what he must do.

The January Convention was scheduled to begin that week at Elim Tabernacle in Rochester. Its joyous, worshipful atmosphere was just what he needed. They would attend, whether they could afford it or not.

They arrived at the tabernacle the next day to find the gloom of death settled upon the company. Their beloved leader, Mrs. Baker, had suffered a stroke, and only hours later, with glory lighting her face, had joined her bridegroom Lord. The convention had begun on the heels of the funeral, with attendance made up largely of those who had come early for the funeral. The sense of loss was oppressive, and only the Holy Spirit's comforting presence rescued the convention from total loss. As Ivan sat stunned with the news, a question loomed demandingly in his mind—"Who can take her place?" His consternation mounted as he listened numbly to a tribute paid her by a guest speaker who spoke of her fidelity to truth, and power to set it forth; of the keenness of her mind to detect error in doctrine; of her worldwide influence through missions, and of the large number of young people filled with the Spirit and trained under her influence to spread the full Gospel all over the world.

The words and moments were traumatic for Ivan. Memories set his pulse to racing—the flaming letters of "REVIVAL" returned to fire his soul. Mrs. Baker's student of two years past stood looking up at the chariot. Could the falling mantle send him forth as a modern Elisha? And the miracles—hadn't he seen many miracles right here in this place? And had he not returned to Elim to receive that mantle of power his soul craved for his own ministry?

"Who can take her place?" The question haunted him. True, there was Susan Duncan on the platform, obviously the future leader of Elim, though stricken this day by the sudden loss that grieved them all. As head of RBTS, she would continue to be highly respected for her brilliant teaching ministry and dominant leadership qualities. But it was Mrs. Baker they had loved for her unfailing kindness to all, for her gentle disposition, her openheartedness, her ability to weigh matters calmly and wisely. Her words of counsel never held a narrow or bigoted statement. There could be no generation gap with such a spirit. As Elijah to Elisha, such had been the relationship of Mrs. Baker to her students. Ivan was deeply stirred. When he and Minnie, similarly impressed, returned to their Reading Center parish, they were determined that the mantle should go into effect—that the message of their departed leader should live on through their ministries.

But one Sunday morning, after preaching an inspired sermon on divine healing, Ivan was approached by the head deacon.

"We appreciate your earnestness, young man, and your desire to be helpful; but we must ask that you confine your sermons to Methodist truths."

Ivan was stunned to silence. The deacon walked away.

The rejection of his message on divine healing that Sunday morning in his first parish was timed with the arrival of the Elim *Trust* magazine. It contained an article describing the acute need of workers to assist the Slocums in their work in India. In his panic over the pastoral problem he faced, Ivan concluded that God had closed one door to open another. Suiting action to decision, he resigned his pastorate. They visited among relatives and friends to explain God's leading, sold household goods to complete the amount needed for two one-way tickets, then boarded the train for New York City.

That night, Ivan and Minnie, with two-year-old Carlton and a second child on the way, put up at a missionary rest home, and the next morning, Ivan made his way to the docks to make final arrangements for sailing.

He entered the ticket office with the exhilaration of fresh challenge—India, where he would preach the full Gospel to a disease-ridden people whose acceptance would bring deliverance and healing. REVIVAL would come to India!

It was a confused young man who walked out of the office a short time later with no tickets—refused because he had no organized mission board to guarantee his return fare. Further complications of hazardous travel—World War I was in progress—and uncertain political conditions in India made the situation impossible, the man said. Ivan now faced finding answers for Minnie, friends, and family—and himself.

Because they had no home of their own to return to, and because Minnie needed to be settled quickly, Ivan accepted the first open door of ministry, a mission in nearby Paterson, New Jersey. For the next few months, Ivan sought God's guidance for their lives with a new carefulness and humility. Confusion and defeat gradually gave way to acceptance of God's closed door.

In April, their second child, Mary Elizabeth, was born, to

cheer and comfort the lone little family. She was destined to become a valued helper in the life work of her father.

# 6

*Revival At Last And A Pentecostal Ministry*

Ivan and Minnie were in their sixth month of ministry in the Paterson mission when word came from home of his father's move to a farm on Day Hollow Road, near Endicott, New York. Perhaps it was a new tenderness toward his parents from the recent dealings of God in his life, as well as a sense of duty, that caused Ivan and his family to return to assist them in their new venture. Alice and Merritt gladly welcomed the help, and the joy of having their grandchildren with them. Ivan also worked at the Endicott Johnson Shoe Factory, preaching weekends.

It was not the happiest setup for Ivan and Minnie, however, for the spiritual differences between Ivan and his parents seemed more pronounced than ever. Minnie felt their antagonism keenly one day when Carlton became very ill. She prayed, then praised, but his suffering continued. Ivan came home, and together they claimed the healing promises, still not calling a doctor. With her heart aching for the child, Minnie overheard Alice remark to Merritt in the kitchen, "Don't they love the child? Why don't they call the doctor!" To Minnie, this was too much. She buried her head on Ivan's shoulder and wept—and together, they prayed again.

Carlton recovered, and their faith was strengthened, but Minnie longed for the freedom of a home of her own. Ivan, in turn, longed to be able to supply it for her. Eagerly, he awaited the Lord's direction to a pastorate, watching meanwhile for some indication of a spiritual breakthrough in his father's heart. But there was none.

In this interim period, Ivan resorted to mission work, street meetings, services in homes and schoolhouses, and tent revival campaigns. Always, his message was the full Gospel: salvation through regeneration, a holy walk with God, the infilling of the Spirit for power for service, divine healing through the atonement, Christ's second coming for a Church "without spot or wrinkle." And God confirmed His word with signs following—conversions, healings, baptisms, and transformed lives.

Attendance was always small, for there was much persecution in those days, and the scorn of nominal church members. Street meetings drew a motley crowd of seekers and onlookers, the curious and the critical, the cheerers and jeerers. Discouragement often came in the form of rotten eggs and police antagonism, but Ivan was never known to be a men-pleaser. So he preached on.

Finally, leaving his parents well settled on their new farm, he moved back to the old homestead with Vern, both to help on the farm and to evangelize in his home area. Perhaps, too, Ivan felt that the closed door to both the mission field and to pastoring, was really God pressing him into witness among his own family. It was with a new humility and love that he sought to live Christ among them, even as he sought ways to further preach the Gospel.

One day as Vern and Ivan worked together in the barn, Vern was arguing as usual. Ivan asked, "What makes you want to argue all the time?" Vern answered, "Well, I know if I can get you to talking, I can find out some things." It was only a crumb of encouragement, but Ivan was grateful for it.

A Holiness evangelist was already at work in campaigns in both the Fairview and West Franklin Methodist churches, so Ivan offered his services and became part of an evangelistic team—Minnie being the soloist. Ivan's Pentecostal experience soon became evident. Though the evangelist valued the young man's inspiring contribution to the services, he did not appreciate Pentecostal teaching and even made fun of it. One night he suggested that Minnie in her solo "sing in tongues to show the people what it's like." Such lightness in matters sacred to Ivan and Minnie made continued teamwork impossible, so again Ivan was forced to go it alone—this time, to start meetings in the little Sayles schoolhouse after the church campaigns had closed.

The schoolhouse meetings were already into the second week before the break came for which Ivan was watching. The winter night was a bitter one, but the potbellied stove amply heated the crowded little room. Lamplight flickered fitfully over the scene inside the schoolhouse—of country folk seated at desks and on benches against the walls, and children snuggled sleepily among them. Outside, horses hitched to sleighs stomped in the snow and nuzzled one another, patiently waiting the service out. The smell of sweat, of kerosene lamps, and farm soil on muddied boots all blended unpleasantly with the acrid smoke that veiled the room and stung the eyes.

The young preacher up front was speaking now with special earnestness. Minnie noticed from where she sat near the door that backs straightened and heads went up as her husband grew more intense in his appeal. And the appeal tonight was not only for repentance and confession of sin, but for a surrender to God that would allow His Holy Spirit to come in, revealing the Christ, and speaking through them in a miracle of unknown language.

It was only hours before the service that Ivan had decided

to preach in this way. He had been in the barn milking—often his best time for communion with God—and had cried out to God in desperation, "Why, God, do You not pour out Your Spirit?"

God had answered with another question. "Well, do you believe that tongues is the evidence of the Baptism in the Spirit?" Ivan thought about this. RBTS had not taught this specifically, and his teamwork with the Holiness evangelist had discouraged his emphasizing it, but God was facing him with it, and he must question it no longer.

"Yes, Lord, I do believe that tongues is the evidence of the Baptism," he answered. The Lord said, "Preach it, then!"

So it was that Ivan was preaching the Baptism in the Spirit with speaking in tongues to his congregation of farmer folk. The room was too crowded for an altar call, so Ivan challenged them to respond to the invitation for salvation right where they were; then to receive the Baptism by yielding to the Spirit right where they sat at their desks. Minnie watched with amazement as all around the room, heads dropped and tears slid down cheeks. A woman near her, Minnie McCain, shoulders shaking with sobs, dropped her head on the desk and sobbed aloud. Quickly, Minnie slipped out of her seat to pray with the woman, thinking as she did of how differently their paths had led—her own, a pleasant love-filled path, the other Minnie's a life of unrelieved care for a full-grown imbecile child, not her own, whose only sounds were like those of a dog. The fifty-year-old woman's past was shrouded in mystery, but the present, Minnie thought, as she slipped her arm around her, promised a brighter future.

Together, the two Minnies wept, then prayed, and before the evening had passed, Minnie McCain was born again and filled with the Spirit. So were others in the room, among them Ivan's sister-in-law, Flora, Vern's wife.

The news spread, attendance increased, and night after

night, people were saved and baptized in the Spirit, speaking in tongues as the Spirit gave utterance.

There were still those who scorned. There was the night when a sleighload of people en route from town stopped in to see what the meeting was all about. They joined the congregation in singing a familiar old hymn. A farmhand of their group, German in nationality, recognized the hymn tune and joined in with the others, singing in German. He was at first puzzled, then amused, when the folk who sat near enough to hear him cried excitedly, "Glory to God, he's got it—the Spirit's in him!"

But that something was happening in the little schoolhouse, no one could doubt, and it was later said that at every farm along the schoolhouse road, if you called out "Praise the Lord," you'd get a "Hallelujah!" in response. Many of these folk, unable to squeeze into the crowded schoolroom, made an altar in their barns or homes and found God there. Often there were testimonies of shaking under the power of God as they sought Him in their homes. But Vern was still among the unsaved.

From this revival, there were the makings of a Pentecostal church for the area, but it did not materialize. Perhaps Ivan felt that a new church might displease his home church pastor and congregation; or perhaps he felt the revival could continue from within the church, through those who had been revived. Whatever the reason, he left Vern's, assured that God had ministry for him elsewhere. They moved to Elmira, where they lived with Uncle Elwin while seeking God for further guidance.

One day, Ivan took Carlton and walked downtown on an errand. Carlton, then only four years of age, asked, "Daddy, hadn't we ought to start some meetings here?" Ivan smiled at his son's early sense of involvement, but the idea stayed with him. After prayer and confirmation from a resident Pentecostal family, he decided it to be indeed God's will.

Together, they opened a mission, renting a downstairs hall and an apartment overhead for their living quarters. Though there was no such outpouring of the Spirit as they had seen at the little Sayles schoolhouse, God nevertheless moved—saving, filling, healing. Two strong churches today are the fruit of this mission.

Another daughter, Eva Adora, was born to the Spencers in February of 1919. The birth was preceded with fear and much prayer, for a polio epidemic in the city was claiming the lives of many pregnant mothers. The normal healthy birth was therefore a cause for much rejoicing. Uncle Elwin and Aunt Lizzie hovered over the crib with loving attention, and Ivan and Minnie were happy with their growing family. How could any of them know that with the passing of years, that little life would bear the bread of life to dark-skinned Morani warriors, of the fierce Masai tribe of East Africa!

There was financial stress, too. It seemed the small offerings were never enough to cover the living expenses of the little family, and rent for the modest quarters.

One evening, Ivan and Minnie knelt to commit to God their immediate need of twenty dollars for the rent. They were weary from the continuous struggle with insufficient finances, and it wasn't easy to close their prayer with praise—but they did. What a joy to receive in the next morning's mail a twenty-dollar check—all the way from a missionary friend in Africa—payment in advance for a favor asked of them.

Not satisfied to minister to one group only, Ivan rented a tent and conducted services in the nearby city of Bath. When the tent campaign closed, home meetings continued, while Ivan moved the tent to Hornell for more services. Again God blessed. Minnie's lovely solos and behind-the-scenes intercession were indispensable to the success of the services, which Ivan was quick to admit. This tent campaign also developed into established home meetings, and Ivan moved to Hornell to pastor the growing congregation. He built a church at the foot of the hill on which the Steuben Sanatorium stood.

The meetings continued in revival power. In a Methodist church in a nearby town, a young man received a spiritual experience that caused him to hunger for more of God. In his search, he was directed to an evangelistic campaign being conducted in the Hornell Methodist Church. He and his wife arrived at the Hornell Pentecostal Church by mistake, not realizing it until after the service had begun. Here they were introduced to a new way of worship that immediately won Alvin Hungerford's heart. His wife Dora was more conservative and at first resisted, but she also felt drawn back to the new little church. Soon both had received the Holy Spirit, and they became fast friends of the Spencers.

It was at this time that Ivan was approached by officials of a new Pentecostal organization and invited to join their fellowship. Ever hungry for fellowship, Ivan gladly filled out the papers which made him a member of the Assemblies of God.

Two more sons were born to Ivan and Minnie during their happy Hornell pastorate—Merritt Worthy in 1921, and Paul Eugene in 1923.

It was inevitable that Ivan and Minnie would have discipline problems in their home—their children were PKs, preacher's kids! Nor did they always agree on the form of discipline to be taken. "Uncle Percy" described their differences in this manner: "Ivan raised the children under law, and Minnie under grace!"

One Sunday morning during the service, the irrepressible Carlton came under his father's law. He was ordered to sit on the front edge of the platform, near his dad.

He sat there in shame, hanging his head, as his father announced the guest preacher, and the sermon began. Down in the congregation, Minnie watched her son's embarrassment in pain, praying he'd not be adversely affected by the ignominious punishment. Carlton's shame deepened when the preacher referred to the "goat" nations—gesticulating with pointed finger in his direction each time he scornfully referred to the "goats."

After three blessed years of pastoring the Hornell congregation, Ivan was invited to the pulpit of a little mission in the thriving industrial community of Endicott. Here they lived with his parents on their farm until a building could be found for a parsonage. The little mission congregation grew, and Ivan led in its being "set in order" with a stated membership and officers. it was his joy to add to the membership list the names of his beloved mother, Alice Spencer, and Minnie's father, Worthy Back, who again lived with them. Joining the church also were David Wellard and Douglas Scott, both ministers and chums from his RBTS days. Now Ivan, though essentially a loner up to this point, began to experience the joy of teamwork with men of God who shared his vision for revival ministry.

Numbers were never a concern with Ivan, and once again, the sparsely settled rural area, with its empty churches and schoolhouses, challenged him. He longed to bring his neighbor farmers into the fullness of salvation that he knew. His sermons, so filled with illustrations from country living, were peculiarly adapted to the spiritual needs of his fellow farmers.

One wintry Sunday afternoon, Ivan labored through blizzard winds and snowdrifts to reach the little Boswell Hill schoolhouse where his service was scheduled. He arrived to find the place empty and cold. Muscles ached from the strain of fighting the drifts, and his heart ached over the indifference of the farm folk and the seeming fruitlessness of his ministry among them. As he went to his knees in prayer, he recalled the promise of earlier days when God had found him on the cornhusk pile and called him to preach—then later at RBTS when God had faced him with flaming letters of "REVIVAL" and fired his soul with a zeal that never dimmed. But now—

Then God spoke. *I want you to open a training school for young people for the supernatural ministry of the last hour.*

How long Ivan lay in God's presence on the cold schoolroom floor, he did not know. But he arose permeated with a new sense of divine commission.

That spring, news reached Ivan that the Rochester Bible Training School had closed. The hour had come for his life work to begin.

# 7

*Elim Bible Institute Is Born—Struggle To Exist*

Elim Bible Institute came to birth during the summer of 1924, in Endwell, New York.

Birthpangs are never easy, and for Ivan Spencer and his little Pentecostal congregation, who were already struggling to maintain a mission ministry to Endicott's industrial community, the beginning of a training center was a difficult challenge. But visionaries do not operate on "things that are seen," and the small congregation and their pastor moved "as seeing Him who is invisible," in obedience to God's call.

"And the Lord worked with them, confirming the word with signs following"—the "sign" in this case being the sacrifice of Alvin and Dora Hungerford who had been flooded out earlier that spring and had sold their property. God dealt with them to give $500 of the money as a down payment toward the purchase of a Bible school facility. Ivan prayed with them regarding their offer and sensed behind it a sincere dedication to identify with him in the new venture. He gladly accepted their help as God's provision.

With their home sold, the Hungerfords moved to Endicott. Day after day, Ivan and Alvin looked for a suitable building—and found nothing. Living in makeshift quarters wasn't easy for the Hungerfords, and one day a good buy on a home was offered them. It seemed God had refused their sacrifice. It was all so confusing. They went to prayer, and Ivan arose with the suggestion, "We've given this money to the Lord. Let us go out to look just one more time."

This time they found it—an old summer clubhouse in the small community of Endwell, bordering Endicott. It was surrounded with fields and woods, and sloped toward the willow-bordered Susquehanna River. They moved in and began the necessary repairs. At the same time, they pitched a large tent for a camp meeting.

A great and blessed time it was, with Charles Shreve, a Spirit-filled Methodist minister from Washington, D.C., as the camp meeting speaker. Assisting him at the piano was Benjamin Baur, an RBTS graduate who later became pastor of the Elim Tabernacle, serving for over forty years. Joe Elliot served capably as song leader. The Holy Spirit moved in glorious ways, among both adults and children, and little five-year-old Eva was filled with the Spirit.

One evening, Minnie put the children to bed as usual, before the night service, so they could get their sleep. The tent was nearby, and eight-year-old Mary lay in her bed listening as Benjamin Baur played in his unusual anointed style, "Nor silver nor gold hath obtained my redemption." The beauty of the music caused her to yearn greatly to play even as he played. The hymn being a familiar one, she followed the music in her mind with the words, and suddenly they gripped her young heart. She burst into sobs, and years later, realized that in that moment God had laid His hand on her for an anointed ministry in music.

"The slain of the Lord were many," and attendance grew as the work of the Spirit was noised abroad. Both Pentecostal and denominational ministers attended with their church youth. There was little advertising, but the tent filled nightly with community folk. Twelve families came to Christ and became part of the little assembly.

One day local antagonism erupted when a group of rowdy youth forcibly dragged Ivan from the tent out into the field and threatened him with harm if the meetings continued. The following day, a stranger stepped up to Ivan on the street and said, "You have nothing to fear, Mr. Spencer; we will see to that." Then he was gone. There was no further trouble, and the presence of the Lord reigned. It was truly a glorious beginning—a fitting dedication of the new Elim Bible Institute, at first called Elim Bible Training School.

That first year, the only campus building was the twelve-room clubhouse into which both students and staff crowded. The Ivan Spencer family occupied one upstairs room, curtained off for privacy from the students who had to pass through to get to their rooms beyond. A married student couple, the Robert Bressettes, and all the single students occupied the other upstairs rooms—along with a printing press. The Hungerfords, also students, had a one-room apartment downstairs. There was also a chapel—which doubled as lecture hall and sanctuary for the local congregation—a dining room, kitchen, and sun porch.

The school opened in November, with a dozen boarding and day students. Most students came trusting the Lord for provision, as did the staff, who were not salaried. A young member of the local congregation, Eva Watson, who worked at the shoe factory office, assisted Minnie with the family in her spare time. She also shared her salary to help out with school needs, and eventually moved into the school.

There was no furnace most of the first winter, but by means of heaters and woodstoves, they managed to survive the bitter winds that blew freely through the walls of the summer structure.

Minnie served as matron of the school, supervising household duties, the dining room and laundry, and doing the buying. She was meticulous, and a firm disciplinarian in managing the students in their work duties. The students considered their household tasks as much a part of Elim's sanctifying discipline as the rules and their studies. A deep respect for Minnie's spiritual stature overrode fears or resentments they might otherwise have held against her.

Classes operated on a flexible schedule, allowing guest teachers the time needed for special teaching emphases. David Wellard, by this time a pastor in Syracuse, taught on the Tabernacle of the Old Testament; William Pocock of Toronto taught on the anointing and gifts of the Spirit, as did Harry Long of Rochester. In the spring, Harold Cornish conducted revival meetings for the community in the little school chapel, with gratifying results in conversions and baptisms. The Vern Spencers also visited the school that first year.

Sports and social life were negligible in Elim's first years, exercise being gotten through hard work, and fun through dorm pranks which would erupt at times from otherwise serious-minded students.

Outreach ministry for the students came through home meetings, cooperation with Clyde Walton's mission in Binghamton, Reverend Conklin's Holiness Church in Owego, door-to-door evangelism in the community, and in street meetings conducted in front of the shoe factory.

Student diary entries from that first year provide phrases that shed light on Elim's school life in its beginnings:

"Spirit came on class today . . . no teaching." "Wonderful time praising God during the meal." "Brother Spencer preached on faith . . . very strong." "Worked hard on the laundry." "Brother Spencer told students they must go out and call on people, or 'get fired'!" "Got two loads of coal today . . . answer to prayer." "Went to M.E. Church . . . preacher talked on Holy Ghost . . . his way of looking at it." "Several quite sick." "Wonderful praise service through two classes." "Snowing today . . . terrific wind blowing." "Brother Spencer talked on 'revivals' tonight." "Revival fires are surely burning." "Altar full of seekers, praying until 2:30 A.M. " "No tables set for dinner . . . fasting and prayer instead." "Three saved in altar service." "Baptist minister came through to the Baptism this afternoon."

It was about this time, in April, 1925, that Minnie, exhausted from her many duties, contracted the grippe which became pleural pneumonia. As she lay in the crowded noisy room that was "home," her condition worsened and her fever mounted dangerously. A splitting headache made every footstep an irritation, while the clanking of the press across the hall was unbearable. The special services being conducted in the downstairs chapel, however, brought solacing sounds of prayer and praise including special prayer for her.

Then God spoke to her of a minister in Owego for whom she felt little respect due to his antagonism to the Pentecostal message. "Send for him to come and pray for you," the Spirit urged. Minnie knew God's voice and felt the request to be a discipline from the Lord for her uncharitable attitude.

Ivan returned with Reverend Conklin, and they prayed and committed her to God's care. Ivan, exhausted from his nightly vigils and the responsibilities of school and revival meetings, fell asleep. He awoke hours later to find his wife worse, her fever higher. As he cried out to God, he saw in the corner of the room what he sensed to be the death angel.

Immediately, he arose in the Spirit and cried aloud, "I rebuke you, death angel, in the name of Jesus. Go!" And the being disappeared. The remainder of the night, Ivan watched Minnie regain her normal breathing and color, and in the morning, she was on the mend. Though she lost all her

64

lovely hair through the ordeal, she rejoiced in her deliverance— and her hair grew in again.

No, birthpangs are not easy, but oh, the joy of holding a husky infant in your arms, of raising that child to manhood and watching God fulfill His purposes through him. Ivan and Minnie had become the spiritual parents of a ministry that was born in the health and bloom of the Spirit, and continued to grow in fulfillment of divine purpose, with the hand of God upon it.

In the summer of 1925, with the cooperation of pastors and churches in the area, a crude tabernacle was built, and a second camp meeting was held—again blessed by an outpouring of God's Spirit. Among those cooperating that summer were J. Roswell Flower and his church of Scranton, Pennsylvania, and Miss Mary Hastie and group from Avoca, Pennsylvania, whose home meetings were the scene of many denominational and Catholic people receiving salvation and the fullness of the Spirit. Bertha Dommermuth of Avoca, who later became Elim's first missionary, says of her contact with Elim at this time:

"The camp meeting was marvelous. . . . Brother Cornish was speaker and gave such anointed messages. . . . The singing was so beautiful—a lot of singing in the Spirit."

Fellowship with the whole Body of Christ was important to Ivan, whose vision of Body ministry extended beyond denominational boundaries. His emphases upon the Baptism in the Spirit and the gifts of the Spirit as being placed in the Body, the Church, rather than given to the individual for personal edification, necessitated that he consider himself a member of the Church universal. He also thought of the school as being the property and ministry of the whole Body of Christ. The quatrain, later adapted on Elim's letterhead, was truly his conviction from the beginning: "The whole Christ, our sufficiency; the whole Bible, our textbook; the whole Church, our fellowship; the whole world, our parish."

Joining the staff that second year were Hazel Fairchild, who had taught at Beulah Heights Bible School in New Jersey; David Wellard, commuting from Syracuse, and Emma Womble—all RBTS graduates. Two homes nearby were rented to house the men students, the Spencer family, and Minnie's father, Worthy Back. But even with these acquisitions, the facilities were crowded, and their prayer for the third year was, "Lord, choose for us the students You wish to come."

Before the second year closed, Ivan's mother, Alice, passed away, and Ivan and his family moved out to Day Hollow to assist in caring for his father and the farm. His brother Leslie had married, bought a piece of his father's farm, and built his home on it. Merritt lived at times with Leslie and his family.

Though the Ivan Spencers' move relieved the crowded conditions at the school, it created a difficult commuting problem. One report states, "Ivan drove, when his Model T wasn't being pushed!"

In late fall, the beginning of the third and last year at Endwell, another death took place at the Day Hollow Farm. Ivan had driven into Endwell, and as it happened, only Carlton and an elderly lady visitor were in the house with Minnie. She was busy in another part of the house, and Carlton, home from school with a broken wrist, had curled up with a book beside the stove in the kitchen. The door opened to admit father Back. He deposited the mail on the kitchen table and turned to warm his hands by the fire, when suddenly he toppled and fell across Carlton—dead! To Carlton, an impressionable young boy, it was a horrifying shock, as it was to Minnie who came running at Carlton's screams. She sent Carlton racing across to Leslie's for help.

Since Leslie was not home, it was Merritt who returned to help and comfort his grieving daughter-in-law. Carlton stood helplessly by as Minnie and Merritt cared for her father's body. When she left the room for a few minutes, Merritt stood gazing down on the inert body of that Christian gentleman, Worthy Back. Unaware of Carlton's presence, Merritt sadly shook his head, muttering, "Oh, if I only knew what he knows now!"

Carlton never forgot the contrast between his two grandfathers—one, only a nominal Christian, the other, a transformed life. But a mellowing process began in Merritt's heart that day—even his grandchildren noticed his new gentleness with them. To Ivan and Minnie, whose hearts were still sore over the loss of mother Alice, this second death hit hard—but Merritt's change in the days that followed brought joy to their hearts. It was answer to prayer and a particular joy to Ivan.

After the third crowded year at Endwell, Ivan began to look about for more suitable facilities. Then came an invitation from the beloved Duncan sisters to move the growing school to Rochester, into a new property which they would purchase for it. With nostalgic thoughts of former blessings, and knowing that a move must be made, Ivan prayed much about it, then accepted the invitation. The *Trust* magazine carried announcements of the school's opening in Rochester:

[*March-April, 1927*]

### Bible Training School Opening

God has revealed a plan by which we are to have a Bible School again in Rochester. Rev. Ivan Spencer, who is one of our student graduates as well as ordained to the ministry, was led to open a school in Endwell, N.Y., as we closed in Rochester. They . . . have outgrown their present quarters and after much prayer and consideration are being definitely led of the Lord to remove their school to Rochester, and will carry on the Bible School in full fellowship with us and with our hearty cooperation.

While the training school will thus be under new management, it will be carried on after the order of the original Elim work . . . . It is not too soon to pray for a repetition of those all-glorious days, such as were experienced at the opening of the old Bible school.

*[July-August, 1927]*

We did not realize that God had one of His servants in training whom He intended bringing forth at the right moment, to take up the work again. . . . That moment has come and Pastor Spencer is now located in our midst.

So it was that Old Elim merged with the new, the two Duncan sisters dreaming of RBTS carrying on as before. Susan Duncan's teaching ministry lent an appreciated richness to the school's curriculum, and her presence drew to the school some of the old Elim associates. The new school location included a spacious colonial home and a large brick carriage house, renovated into a dormitory, classrooms, and a chapel which the Duncan sisters purposed would replace the Elim Tabernacle and make the new Elim independent of other churches in the city. They planned to continue being the headquarters of conventions, and to disregard such activities by other churches.

It was soon obvious that all things were not as they had been when Mrs. Baker was the cohesive force. Some years after her death, and upon the school's closing, the Elim Tabernacle congregation had joined the Assemblies of God, against Susan Duncan's wishes. She and her sisters, and others who felt as she did about "organization," pulled away, selling the property to the congregation, but retaining the

Elim home and the print shop. It was with this money that she had bought the property for the new Elim school.

Ivan had been enjoying fellowship with all the churches in Rochester up to this point and could not see breaking fellowship now, even though to continue in fellowship with the others meant pressures in the operation of the school. Before long, the strain began to tell on their friendship with the Duncan sisters.

One Sunday as Minnie hurried toward the church for service, a carload of friends who were driving by en route to the Elim Tabernacle stopped to chat with her. After a few minutes, they drove on, and Minnie hurried into the church. Immediately, she noted trouble signs—whispering that ceased when she drew near, and cold, disapproving looks. Her chat with friends outside was being interpreted as disloyalty and troublemaking.

Such tensions came at a bad time for Minnie, for she was again pregnant, the baby being due that month. She was irritated and impatient with the situation. Then their salary was withheld, and their conditions worsened. The rented home which their family, with three students, occupied next to the school, had to be given up. Into one large room the Spencer family of seven moved, Carlton sleeping in his father's office. They ate with the students in a crowded dining room, endeavoring to maintain a rejoicing attitude for the sake of the students.

But Minnie's heart was broken, and her ministry of intercession often laid her low on the carpet of their one-room home, weeping and groaning in an agony of prayer for a spiritual breakthrough. Also sad and distraught, Ivan would often join her in her prayer vigils. He was dismayed at the situation in which the school found itself, but arose each time from prayer with a strengthened conviction that he dare not compromise his vision of Churchwide fellowship, regardless of the cost.

Quite possibly, the "cost" was magnified by Ivan's adamant refusal to recognize the sisters' right to interfere in this activity of the school. After all, they had initiated the invitation and provided the property. Whether right or wrong, it was Ivan's uncompromising attitude on the issue of open fellowship that precipitated the crisis, and both sides suffered as they sought to learn the ways of God.

Then the baby arrived—a fine baby girl, Ruth Minnie. Oh the magic of a newborn babe! To the students, living under a pall of concern and tension, the baby's presence was a joyous relief and called for a celebration. The next day, Minnie's door swung open to admit a jolly group of students pushing a new crib, which they had united in purchasing. To Ivan and Minnie, their loving expression was a "balm in Gilead," and made the advent of their new little one just a bit more welcome. But their gift made even more noticeable the lack of any expression of interest from the still revered Duncan sisters.

There was the occasion when an evangelist, a mutual friend of the Spencers and Duncans, was invited by Susan to take the pulpit one Sunday. The message on rebellion against leaders became excruciating to Ivan as he realized the intent of the sermon.

Then one Sunday morning when Pastor Ivan and family arrived at the church, he found himself replaced by his dear missionary friends, the Albert Slocums of India, recalled from the field for the purpose of filling the pastoral "vacancy." Ivan and Minnie, with the children, sat in the back pew that morning, heartsick and convinced that the school would have to move.

How could it be that God would allow all this division and heartbreak over a simple act of fellowship with others of the Body of Christ? Little did Ivan and Minnie realize that this crucifixion was leading to a resurrection—a loosing from the perpetuation of another's vision (that had already beautifully

70

fulfilled its purpose in God's plan) into the freedom necessary to fulfill God's purpose for them—that of training youth for endtime revival, in a fellowship that would know no boundaries.

But how could they move—and where? Operating by faith had given them no treasury reserve, nor did they have property. (They had given the Endwell investment to the local church; their Rochester facility was owned by the Duncan sisters.)

Then an appropriate building was found fifty miles away, in Red Creek, New York. It was an old academy, deteriorating but potentially useful after cleaning and repair. Again God provided the $500 down payment needed through the sacrifice of a student. The move was made, as the one from Endwell had been, in a small antiquated truck.

For young Carlton, now a teenager making his way through high school, the work of the ministry had paled. The ardor with which he had viewed his father's work in Elmira days, had reversed to become an embarrassment. Deeply affected by the bitter ordeal through which his parents had just passed, he also suffered disillusionment. Obedient to his father's orders, he had worked at his side in the school's resettlement, but he resented it. His bitterness only increased when he enrolled that fall in the Red Creek High School, and was taunted for being a holy roller. The lot of a PK (preacher's kid) was not an easy one.

But for Ivan and Minnie, just being in their own quarters again, free to pursue God's will for their fledgling school, was a joy.

# 8

*The Willow Flourishes, Then Withers*

The move to Red Creek completed, Ivan and Minnie faced this new phase of their ministry with a more disciplined faith. They were finding that "any dead fish can float downstream; it takes a live one to swim upstream." They were weary. This was their third attempt in five years to carry on a training school for revival ministry. In each case, there was much physical labor involved. Ivan had become carpenter, plumber, and electrician, as well as administrator, teacher, and preacher—and always there was farming to do, to supplement the food budget.

Again they pitched a large tent—for their fourth camp meeting. (The move to Rochester had precluded a camp the previous summer.) Certain brethren were conspicuous for their absence that summer, due to misunderstanding of the division at Rochester. But though the absence of some was noticeable, God sent in new ones whose ministries blessed the camp.

School opened in October on a high tide spiritually. On the teaching staff that year were Ivan Spencer, Emma Womble, Mrs. G.R. Niles, Adolphus Smith, and Lillian

Nitsch—graduates of the previous year—and Frank Finkenbinder, a missionary home on furlough from Puerto Rico
(father of the well-known Paul Finkenbinder of Central
America).
time—Bible Atlas and Missions, with Missionary Prayers as
part of the daily schedule. In a printed report, dated 1929, a
student describes what school life was like at Red Creek that
first year:

> Many times the Spirit falls as the blessing is asked at
> the dining tables. . . . One Sunday morning service,
> many were prostrated under the power of the Spirit,
> others dancing in the Spirit, and all glorifying God.
> The Lord spoke to many hearts. . . . Sunday
> afternoons some pray, others gather to sing, still
> others go out to do personal work among the shut-ins.
> . . . Each night of the week we have prayers for a
> special country, but Sunday evenings we pray for the
> homeland and its needs. . . . One Sunday night
> service lasted until after 5:00 the next morning, the
> tarrying service being one in which the Lord truly had
> His way. . . . As a rule lights are out at 10:00 P.M. The
> daily schedule usually begins at 6:30 bugle call to
> arise, dress for breakfast and enjoy a half-hour private
> devotional time. After breakfast is the 8:00 A.M.
> worship in the lecture room. A student usually is in
> charge to bring something from the Word—singing
> and prayer requests are included. Duties follow which
> include: care of the dining room—two students are
> waitresses; vegetable preparation; dishes and pots and
> pans; cleaning of halls, stairs and lecture room,
> library, etc. At 9:45 A.M. classes begin with a bell and
> continue until lunchtime at 12:00 noon. Worship
> around the tables precedes lunch, with compulsory
> recreation following lunch, from 1:00 to 3:00 P.M.

Study from 3:00 P.M. to 5:00 P.M., with Missionary Prayers immediately following. From 7:30 to 9:30 P.M. is study again, then to bed at 10:00 P.M.

The backing of certain pastors and friends continued to drop off, some of this due to the geographic isolation of the new school. Lack of finances became a daily hassle, and only through extreme budgeting and the exercise of thrift in countless ways could they continue. Minnie rose to the occasion, providing meals for her family of fifty-plus on a shoestring. Ivan sent Carlton out day after day to pick up coal along the railroad tracks. A cow was purchased and chickens raised to supply milk and eggs. The second summer, a garden was planted to supply the table for the coming winter. Arrangements were made with a farmer, and his woodlot provided a substitute for expensive coal, but not without an added burden of work on Ivan and his student helpers. Carlton was glad, however, to be through with the embarrassing job of scrounging for coal along the tracks. The task may have had exercise value, but it engendered in him a smoldering resentment for school and students—and life in general.

Again the tent was pitched for camp meeting. With more new contacts replacing the dwindling backing of old friends, Ivan and Minnie suffered the pressures of a transition period, both in fellowship and in the Spirit's move among them. But God honored the preaching of His Word with His presence and power, in spite of their weariness and ill-timed personal family problems.

One personal concern which came to a head that first week of camp meeting, was Carlton's increasing spiritual indifference. The crisis was precipitated by his attendance at a rodeo against his father's wishes.

In the busyness of camp administration and the services, Ivan was unable to give the boy his undivided attention, for either counsel or discipline. In the few moments he had for the unpleasant confrontation with his unrepentant son, he issued his debatable ultimatum. "Shall I give you a sound thrashing, or shall I make you attend every camp meeting service?"

Carlton considered, then chose to attend the services.

"All right," his father declared in iron tones. "You shall be in every service for the remainder of this camp meeting. I shall be looking for you!"

For a restless, disinterested teenager, it was a rugged assignment—and a resented one. Carlton knew he must obey his father, and he did. However, his father's preoccupation with the progress of the services allowed Carlton to smuggle in his favorite magazines to read during the sermons—and even at the altar where his presence was expected.

As to the wisdom of such discipline we will not judge. Suffice it to say that Ivan backed such a measure with his concern and prayers, Minnie also interceding on Carlton's behalf—and with their discipline and prayers together they bound Carlton to the will of God.

Another personal trial that came during that second camp meeting at Red Creek was the sickness of their baby daughter Ruth. When her pains and fever increased, Minnie and Eva Watson spelled each other in a prayer vigil at her bedside, meanwhile trying to care for the needs of the camp-meeting crowd. Then Ivan called the congregation to prayer. Still no answer. As the days passed, an old man who lived on campus and worked for the school, though not a Christian, took his turn at the little girl's side. She was a favorite with him, and he longed to see her well.

As Ruth grew worse, he lost patience with Ivan and Minnie because they did not call a doctor. He went about the small community expressing his anger and his anxiety for the little girl "up thar with them holy-rollers."

The town's indignation reached Ivan's ears, and they all

sought the Lord even more earnestly for His healing power to be manifest. What a delight and relief soon after to note the child's improvement, to the extent that she attended the services the last few days. But it had been a wearisome vigil for the already overtaxed parents, and they were well aware of the town's displeasure over the incident.

School began that fall with an increase of students—and work. Ivan was increasingly concerned over the lack of balance between a cloistered study and worship life, and practical ministry to outside needs. Student ministry outreach in this new location was limited, though his contacts with area churches and his beginning pastorate of a little church in Watertown had inserted wedges that would make openings for future student ministry. The efforts of the students to blend with the community and its churches exposed them to the criticism of the uninitiated to Pentecostal meetings. The students often felt squelched as they returned to the school, and gave voice to their concern in classroom discussions.

On one such occasion, Ivan's reaction was a slow smile and twinkle, a thoughtful rub of his nose in typical gesture, then words of wisdom that revealed the objectiveness with which he at first handled his own problem.

"Criticism is like the cold water that Elijah caused to be poured upon his sacrifice on Mount Carmel. It hinders the fire from getting out and doing any damage in great drought; and it also keeps out any strange fire. The 'strange fires' of error and our own natural energies and emotions do get on the altar of God. The Lord allows the cold water of false report and criticism to cause us to search our hearts; to see if our fire is strange fire, or the real fire of God." Then, lifting his face heavenward, forgetful of watching students, he prayed with all earnestness, "In spite of what it costs, dear Lord, give us the real Baptism of the Holy Ghost and fire."

After a few moments he continued, "A young preacher

76

once asked John Wesley's advice on how to get a good congregation. His answer was, 'Get on fire and the people will come to watch you burn!' May it be said of Elim Bible Institute that the Lord is there, so that any who need God may know where they can find that need satisfied."

Ivan's questing heart led him into progressive revelation of truth; truths that at times came from a personal experience that would drive him to seek God with an open Bible and questioning heart. Such had been the occasion when he received his revelation on the gifts of the Spirit. Needs in the work had driven him to seek the gifts for himself, in order to meet the needs. God showed him His superior plan of Body Ministry—each member of the Body of Christ operating in the Spirit to meet needs as the Spirit moved among them. The gifts were thus the property of the Body of Christ collectively, rather than individually owned and operated, independent of the Body.

This was God's plan, and Ivan could see in it a safety, and a unifying process that delighted him with its potential for a new realm of fellowship.

Then also, revelation would come through outside ministries, as he would listen openly, sifting the message by the Word. Such came to Ivan and Elim at this time, concerning the grace of God.

As the year progressed, Ivan noticed an unwholesome introversion in their seeking of God for death to the self-life, in preparation for attaining "Brideship." Theologically, he had a strong Arminian background, and he realized he had conveyed an imbalance to the students with his challenge to holiness. At this time, a magazine was coming to their address, *Grace and Glory*, from a strongly Calvinistic group in Kansas City, Missouri. Ivan invited their ministry, and the emphasis upon God's grace was a wholesome revelation of truth to Ivan personally, as well as to the students and staff. Faith, and trust in God's ability beyond their weaknesses, revived their joy in the Lord.

Ivan invited one of the Missouri leaders to join the staff the next year, but his radical emphasis on eternal security, and his aversion to worship in the Spirit, brought not only division among the students, but regrettable criticism from the outside—that Elim had "gone eternal security." The teacher whose views were the more extreme of the "Grace and Glory" group, had to be dismissed to ensure peace and bring back the freedom of the Spirit in class sessions.

All in all, what started as a fresh breeze in the Spirit, remained to become a cyclone of trouble, and Ivan wearied of the seemingly inevitable doctrinal controversies, with their attendant lapses in the Spirit. He was finding there is a price to pay in cultivating fellowship with others of the Body who vary in minor points of doctrine. For even while their emphasis complements your lack, friction can result which can try the patience and demand a loving understanding born only of the Spirit. Ivan was learning a new dependence on the Holy Spirit, not only for the detecting of truth from error, but in the maintaining of balance within the whole body of truth. But he was committed to a fellowship with the whole Body of Christ, regardless of cost.

One day in his quest for an expanded fellowship, Ivan sought God for fresh direction. Surprisingly, the challenge came, "Lengthen thy cords and strengthen thy stakes."

"But how, Lord?" he cried, as he considered one church after another and realized that in none of them would he be welcomed. In answer, God illumined these words in his Bible: "The Lord shall open unto thee His good treasure, the heaven to give rain unto the land in His season, and to bless all the work of thy hand; and thou shalt lend unto many nations, and shalt not borrow . . . and thou shalt be above only and thou shalt not be beneath, if thou hearken unto the commandments of the Lord thy God."

Then God spoke forcibly, with that inner voice: *I am going to give you the Steuben Sanatorium at Hornell, and I want you to go in and possess it.*

Ivan had admired the building as a lovely potential for a Bible school when he had built his church near it. He hadn't forgotten it in these intervening years, but he had never seriously considered it, or prayed about it. However, now God was speaking, and the message came through with quickening power, so Ivan acted. He went, marched about the buildings as Israel did about Jericho, and praised the Lord. But nothing happened—apparently.

Throughout that second year at Red Creek, Ivan's utter weariness, his isolation from much of the ministerial fellowship he had previously enjoyed, and the stinging criticisms of those he cherished as spiritual leaders, caused him to reevaluate and compromise his stand for an unbounded liberty in the Spirit. As he observed the students' carefree abandon in the Spirit, often magnified in manifestations by their natural youthful exuberance, he began to feel that perhaps others were right—that propriety in the realm of spiritual worship was essential to the progress of God's work.

Almost unconsciously, in his leadership of the services, he began to substitute natural activity (that same "strange fire" he had criticized in others) for that alertness to the Spirit's expression which emanates from waiting upon God together in a service. In this way, he could subtly divert students who obviously were being moved upon toward some physical manifestation of the Spirit.

He grew to dread such manifestations, for they pointed up the painful controversy between him and fellow Pentecostal ministers. Through what they felt to be his lack of disciplined leadership, he had allowed extremes that had turned them away. Inevitably, resentment toward these brethren replaced the forgiveness and long-suffering that he had always held toward them. Roots of bitterness began to grow and multiply in his heart.

Physically, Ivan continued to weaken. As to which caused which—the bitter resentment of criticism, and the severe case of sciatica—one cannot know. But Ivan was eventually confined to his bed, and the school struggled on without him. The wood supply dwindled, and farm and maintenance chores were only sketchily done for lack of his capable supervision. He lay on the bed helpless, knowing the shambles that could come if his sickness continued.

The willow no longer followed the river's course; nor did its roots intermingle with the roots of others in the river's depths. The verse, "His leaf also shall not wither, and whatsoever he doeth shall prosper" had lost its luster for Ivan, and was only one more card in his promise box.

The setting sun cast its dim wintry light through the sickroom, reminding Ivan of another day wasted in bed—nothing accomplished in the classroom, outreach ministry, or maintenance work. He groaned in his pain and his distress, then remembered the Israelites about whom he'd often preached, "who first sighed, then cried, then groaned—and it was when they groaned aloud in despair that God heard them." Well, here he, Ivan Spencer, was in similar straits. He had tried to adjust his ministry to gain man's approval, and instead, had become not only foolish in the eyes of man, but in God's sight as well. Would he ever learn? If he cried aloud with groanings, as did Israel, would God hear? In agony of soul, he bared his heart to God—all his ugly resentment and bitterness, and worst of all, his fear, fear that he had missed God's will by what others called foolishness.

God answered, *Child, I have called you to train young people for supernatural ministry—if you'll stand out of My way, I will train them as I move upon them by My Spirit.*

That was all, but it was enough to free Ivan from his fears

of liberty in worship, and his self-imposed duty of policing the Spirit's move among them. Immediately, his condition began to mend.

It was an exuberant and thankful family that welcomed Ivan back into circulation. In that first service, he encouraged the slightest breeze of worship in the Spirit, in an almost feverish attempt to recapture the freedom they had once known. Little by little, the fledglings again tried their wings, and soon were fluttering about, learning to fly in the realm of the supernatural. Ivan watched with chastened spirit and deep gratitude to God.

# 9

*Back To The Watercourses And Ongoing Revival*

When school closed that spring of 1930, Ivan and Minnie still faced extreme spiritual and financial pressures. The school's future looked black indeed, if they did not soon find the backing of others in the Body of Christ.

At the supper table one evening, Ivan and Minnie discussed their situation. Finally Ivan blurted out, "There must be someone, someplace, who can help us!" As he lapsed into a glum silence, Minnie prayed—and then she spoke.

"This Sister Ella Moon's church in Knoxville, Pennsylvania— What we've heard has been encouraging. Could we make a visit there?"

"What with?" Ivan asked gloomily, reminding them both of their penniless condition.

But Minnie's suggestion was the only step in view, so they took it in desperation. Perhaps they remembered the lepers who sat outside the besieged gates of Jerusalem. "Why sit we here until we die?" they had asked, and they found God's provision as they took the risk. And risk it was, for Ivan had gas enough only to get them to Knoxville—and no money!

Their few hours visit in the home of the pastor, and with

the guest preacher, Seeley D. Kinne, was an oasis to their spirits. So impressed was Ivan that he invited both of them to minister at the camp meeting that coming summer. As they left, Sister Moon slipped an offering into his hand that enabled them to make the next visit God had laid on their hearts—one to western Pennsylvania.

On their return across Pennsylvania, they came to the little town of Covington. Here they visited a little old lady who had attended their meetings in Elmira years before, and had received a remarkable healing. They found her still rejoicing in the Lord's goodness. When they rose to leave, she said, "Here take this," and slipped a coin into Minnie's hand. That fifty cents was fresh assurance to Ivan and Minnie of God's hand upon them, for their gas tank was again empty, and this would buy enough gas to take them the rest of the way to Vern's.

When they arrived, after greetings, Vern remarked caustically, "There's a meeting going on at the schoolhouse tonight. You wouldn't want to miss it, of course."

He was right. They wouldn't want to miss it; and neither did his wife, Flora, either—so Vern went along.

Frank Finkenbinder, who had taught the previous year at Red Creek and now taught at Beulah Heights Bible School in New Jersey, was the minister for the services held intermittently since Ivan's revival meeting there years before. For Ivan and Minnie it was a blessed service—a time of warm fellowship with old friends, and also further reassurance of God's care.

Frank had announced to his congregation, "I know we don't usually take up a midweek offering, but I'm sure we want to express our thanks to the Spencers for their ministry, tonight and in the past."

That seven-dollar offering, a sacrifice for simple farmer folk, quite overwhelmed Ivan and Minnie, and they returned to Red Creek with money in their pockets and renewed faith that where God guides, He provides.

Summer camp that year was glorious beyond all previous camps. The richly anointed preaching of Mrs. Moon, Seeley D. Kinne, and C.O. Dickinson—an evangelist from Pennsylvania—brought fresh spiritual challenge. The strong dispensationalist concept of the endtime being only a great falling away and lessening of blessing until Christ returned, was shattered by these anointed messengers. Their revelation and scriptural presentation of endtime revival renewed Ivan's faith in his own revelation years before at RBTS. And Ivan's refreshed and chastened spirit added much to the depth of worship and flow of spiritual gifts.

Other emphases of truth projected by these preachers were "selective rapture," "brideship"—as distinct from the Church—and "the manchild company," referred to in the Book of Revelation. These were not new to Ivan, who had heard them preached at Old Elim, but he opened to them now, and they became an increasing influence upon all his future ministry.

Kinne's teaching on "God's Forward Move" and release from formalism—"present your bodies a living sacrifice"—encouraged the cooperation of all to express themselves freely in worship. From this, there were doubtless some unwise, fleshly manifestations that took place, as well as the blessed and good. But there was a genuine release in worship, and the services went on into the wee hours, night after night, the final service lasting until dawn.

One young man sat watching from a back bench, observing the Spirit's move among the people. Outwardly, he was a typical PK in rebellion, present only because he was required to be. But the obvious reality of God's blessing upon the other young people began to get to him—and he stirred uneasily. Could it be that his dad was right—that worship and ministry in the Spirit was a priority worth suffering for?

As the services progressed, Carlton's hunger for God's

presence in his own life conquered his resentment and rebellion. He joined in earnestly with the other seekers at the altar. One fear remained with him, the fear of facing the taunts of his schoolmates again. Under tremendous conviction, he approached his father about leaving high school and enrolling as an Elim student that fall. He was a music major with a bright future before him. Ivan realized it had to be God for Carlton to make such a request, so he cooperated. It was really not until later that fall, however, that Carlton had a life-changing encounter with the Lord that caused him to enter wholeheartedly into his parents' ministry.

A year earlier, a young lady from Rochester had enrolled at Elim—Elizabeth Garate, the daughter of missionaries to Chile. At that time, Elizabeth was the only enjoyment that Elim offered to Carlton. As the principal's son, he found ways to be around her, and to enjoy that social life so generally missing at Elim. Wherever Elizabeth turned, it seemed, he was there; even in the pantry, on the pretense of getting butter for the table, when her duty took her there to color the margarine and slice the bread. One day they planned together to meet on a certain road at a certain time, and on that day, they enjoyed an uninterrupted visit.

But Elizabeth's joy was tempered by a nagging conscience. She was a student and was disobeying a rule. Before they parted, she knew what she must do.

"Carlton, I've got to confess this. I've broken a rule, and I don't feel good about it."

"Aw, now," he expostulated. "Why d'ya have to do that?" Then, not feeling so good about it himself, he added, "Well, if you feel you must, go ahead."

Later, Elizabeth sought out Minnie in her apartment. It wasn't going to be easy to confess to this paragon of discipline, who also happened to be the mother of her heartthrob.

". . . And I knew I shouldn't, but I did. I-I'm sorry," Elizabeth finished penitently, awaiting the wrath that should come.

"Let's pray about it, Elizabeth," was Minnie's surprising answer, and her prayer was even more disconcerting, as she concluded, "and Lord, if You wish Carlton and Elizabeth to be together, I know You will work it out for them."

Elim had passed an important milestone with the 1930 camp meeting, and school began that fall with an influx of new students and a continuous spirit of revival. With Ivan's encouragement of manifestations of the Spirit, there came a new flow of prophecy, some of which was suited to actions inspired by the Spirit, called "acting prophecy." Reminiscent of the old prophets and of incidents in the early Church, it was a dramatic expression of the Spirit, part of God's multimedia approach in teaching His people.

Already Elim was being known for a freedom in worship that exceeded the norm for Pentecostal churches in that day. A man of the Word, Ivan strictly adhered to scriptural boundaries, but any remonstrances from dissenting pastors regarding the no-noes of propriety, only whetted his appetite the more for worship in the Spirit and spiritual gifts. Some may have considered this preoccupation to be a developing hangup, but at least it kept Elim free from an encroaching formalism that even then was choking out the spiritual life and worship in many a Pentecostal congregation.

There were many firsts for Ivan and Elim that year, an important one being the change from a two-year to a three-year course of study. This had been requested by the students, and after prayer, Ivan felt it to be God's leading. He saw that it would make for a more stable foundation for preparation for ministry.

Too, the first issue of the *Elim Pentecostal Herald* came forth that January, with Ivan Spencer as editor, and Max

Wood Moorhead and Maida Blanchard, associate editors. These last two had joined Elim's staff the past year—Moorhead, a missionary from India with a godly influence that enriched the school in all areas of its ministry; and Miss Blanchard, a Spirit-filled graduate of the Practical Bible Training School of Binghamton, New York, also a valuable staff member as teacher and intercessor.

This first issue of the *Herald* carried the report of God's move in their midst and in the churches, certain camp meeting messages by Kinne, Moon, and Dickinson, and an editorial by Ivan. The format was similar in the issues that followed, including news from the missionfield, and later, world news items and prayer requests.

The *Herald* spread the news of what God was doing and saying at Elim. From its teaching on the restoration of the five ministries to the church—apostles, prophets, evangelists, pastors, teachers—Elim and those in fellowship became known as Restorationists or Forward Movers. Strange name, that—Forward Move—and its actual origin is still a mystery. An Elim graduate of 1957, Robert Johansson, when asked suspiciously if he were a Forward Mover, gave answer, "Which way are you going?"

But what really was the Forward Move—so-called until attention was focused on the Latter Rain movement in the 1940s? In one sense, for Elim, it was what made the Latter Rain movement happen. As cogged wheels mesh to produce the clock's timing, so each new move of the Spirit down through history acts as a cog that moves the wheels of future revival. Thus God's clock of divine intervention strikes again and again to bring each generation back to His great loving heart.

As Seeley Kinne pointed out in the January 1932 issue of the *Herald*, "Nothing has ever met conditions of need in the past but a fresh, new move of God. . . . Many gracious and powerful things given by God to the New Testament church have been lost under the rubbish of superstition and tradition. They are old, but will seem new when brought to the light again. . . . For shame that any who call themselves Pentecostal should decry the efforts to recover them. . . . New inventions fill the world; should God sit still while men progress? . . . It is the hour of the coming of the King to end earth's dark night. The air should be full of glorious revelations . . . new movements and blessings in abundance, till the fulfillment of that glorious prophecy which promises, 'Behold I make all things new.' "

In another sense, the Forward Move was a microcosm of revival itself, from the Upper Room to Azusa Street. It embodied the chief ingredients—in taste and form—of all revivals of all time. Its emphases of truth were wedges into the church's mainstream: for worship in the Spirit as opposed to ritual, for free expression of the Spirit through laity, for a non materialistic mentality, for a holy-life consciousness, for creative and joyous expression of the Spirit in daily life. All this—in sample form only—awaiting development as the Church would become "Body"-conscious and act as an unwalled unity.

In a real sense, Elim pioneered in revival, as have earlier groups in earlier periods of history. And the expression of God was always basically the same—overflowing love, exuberant joy, ecstatic worship, miracle expressions of the Spirit—*charisma!*

The 1931-32 school year opened with the Red Creek facility bursting at the seams. Ivan felt sure God's time was near for a move into larger quarters. He also knew what place it should be—the Steuben Sanatorium. It was vacant now, had been reported as sold, but the sale did not go through. He felt a strong impulse to go and look at it, prayerfully, and to again claim it by faith. He contacted the caretakers, Pentecostal people, who in turn invited him and

Minnie to come for a few days of rest and prayer. By this time, some friends had communicated to him their conviction that Elim should move to the Hornell property, and there had even been prophecies to this effect. But there was one small problem—Ivan did not have the $40,000 cost price (a low one at that). He was not able even to register his car that year, so had no transportation to go and pray over the place.

In February of 1932, borrowing a student's car and two dollars for gas, Ivan and Minnie made the trip to Hornell, past the little Pentecostal church that he had built ten years before, and on up the hill to where the huge brick structure already showed signs of deterioration. With their spiritual antennae up, they walked about the twenty-eight acres of wooded land, noting the spot that would easily accommodate the camp meeting tent and guest campers, the space for a garden, and a shed for the necessary cows and chickens. They passed solemnly through the halls and rooms—five floors with 115 large rooms, adaptable to Bible-school living. Then they together sought God for renewed guidance. It came in the form of prophecy to Ivan himself. The message was detailed and painted a bright picture for their ministry in this very setting. How they enjoyed those anointed days of seeking God together! They returned to Red Creek refreshed in spirit, and assured of the part the building would play in Elim's future.

Arriving home, they called the whole school family together. As the students crowded into the chapel, they heard the jubilant announcement—". . . a lovely building, five floors of rooms—and God wants us to have it!" If the price of $40,000 shocked the students and staff, it didn't daunt their faith, and the weekday prayer services became times of praying and praising God for the Hornell property.

The Elim fellowship family was growing fast, from contacts through the increased study body and readership of the *Herald*, and from a widening circle of pastors and churches interested in the refreshing, evident at the Elim oasis. To accommodate the spiritual thirst of these newcomers, a convention was held that Thanksgiving at Red Creek, the services being conducted in the village theater.

For some inexplicable reason, the services began with an overshadowing of bondage. A group of Polish Pentecostal people from Watertown were present, and one of them, a large stout woman, suddenly stood to her feet and began to stamp. Many were aware that she was in spiritual warfare against the enemy who held the service in bondage. When her manifestation ceased, there was a real spiritual breakthrough, and a freedom that spearheaded a blessed convention. Such unique expressions of spiritual warfare became an Elim distinctive in days to come, though such expressions have always attended any revival in history.

That winter, the glory cloud closed in on the school and churches. The major thrusts of the Spirit throughout the budding fellowship were liberty in worship, restoration teaching, intercessory prayer, and missions, with many and varied supernatural manifestations bearing out these thrusts of truth. The *Herald* cites these, from the Knoxville, Pennsylvania, assembly: "The spiritual worship is glorious . . . playing the piano in the Spirit, with supernatural volume . . . heavenly instruments heard but unseen . . . word of wisdom setting apart several for service . . . healings, conversions and baptisms . . . opposing Baptist deacon baptized . . . glorious visions . . . demons cast out of a little boy and no more convulsions."

Revival did not replace the practical side of Christianity, as proved by the churches' cooperation with the school's material needs. From the beginning, the Lyons Assembly had faithfully showered the school with groceries and produce each Thanksgiving. This warm fellowship was due in part to Ivan's influence in getting the church started some years before. Ivan had been asked for counsel regarding an available investment for pioneering a church. He had shared with the donor his concern for the town of Lyons, and told of an empty church for sale there. The church was opened and a congregation built up through the anointed, faithful ministries of Mrs. Mary Danforth and her spiritually gifted assistant, Miss McClellan. God's blessing rested richly upon the church from the very beginning, and some of Elim's most promising students came from the Lyons Assembly.

These elderly sisters often served Ivan with wise counsel, being recognized prophetesses of the Church. He learned to value the word of the Lord that came through them, but he was hardly prepared for what he received from them one day, when he arrived at their door, dejected over fresh misunderstandings and slights. He poured out his tale of woe, ending with "so you see, I need help."

"I see you need help," declared Miss McClellan frankly, "but what you really want is sympathy!"

Ivan swallowed hard and accepted the rebuke. She said no more, and he needed no more—he had gotten the "help" he needed!

At the school, the Spirit flowed in spontaneous student-initiated prayer meetings, in fresh revelations of truth, in visions. Missionary fervor ran high—thirty-three of the forty-six enrolled claimed a call to some foreign mission field. Many later fulfilled that call and scattered the homefires of revival like so many incendiary bombs—to Africa, China, India, and Europe. In fact, from Elim's first decade, one tenth of her graduates became missionaries—Elim's tithe unto the Lord of the Harvest.

Thus, early in Elim's history, there were former students returning from mission fields, whose shared testimonies to starry-eyed students always brought the balancing comment from their principal, "Remember, the calling of God is not necessarily to be a minister or a missionary; but the call of

God for you is unto God Himself, first of all. Elim is for your preparation to fulfill that call."

It was at this time that an emergency arose over the sending out of a former student missionary to a new field of labor. Bertha Dommermuth had already served in Liberia under another mission board and with their missionaries, but also in association with Elim, then at Endwell. Upon her return to the States, she maintained fellowship with her home group, under the leadership of Miss Mary Hastie of Avoca, Pennsylvania; and also with her alma mater, Elim.

In seeking to go to Ethiopia where the Lord was directing her, Ivan advised that she go out again under the same mission board, that she might have the fellowship of their missionaries. Their letter of response said that they were happy with her work in Liberia and would gladly sponsor her for Ethiopia, *when* she had canceled affiliation with her home group and Elim. This she did not feel she could do.

Elim was therefore pressed into establishing the Elim Full Gospel Association, which included the Elim Foreign Missionary Society (now Elim Fellowship), in connection with the Elim Bible Institute. Their reason for this organization, they stated as follows:

We know of no missionary society which is in full harmony with the convictions, principles, and aims of the Elim Bible Institute. It is our privilege as well as our duty to assist our graduates to reach foreign fields. . . . Operating as we do on faith lines, our prospects are as radiant as the promises of God. Each is expected to trust God for outfit, passage, and maintenance. As fellow members in the Body of Christ, the Elim Missionary Society will stand in faith and prayer with them, and encourage affiliated assemblies to send offerings.

With such a radiant outlook, Elim's first appointed missionaries went forth—and Elim took its first cautious step toward organization, in spite of its strong statements regarding the Church as "an organism, *not* an organization." Though yet further steps must be taken in the future to expedite its God-given call, Elim still maintains today the principle set forth by Ivan Spencer in a declaration by him April, 1931:

It is clearly recognized that the Church today is in a state indescribably inferior to that set forth in the Scriptures. . . . God has recently told us . . . that He will restore the New Testament church in a power and glory exceeding that of Apostolic days. . . . What are we to do with this great promise? Shall we follow the example of Abraham in his unbelief, and add another Ishmael to the long list of organizations? Shall we not, rather, hold steady before the Lord, confidently expecting that He will do what He has promised?

All the great revivals of history have declined, sooner or later, after organizational system crept in. The experience of Christians in all ages has been that organization causes inspired doctrine to degenerate into the dogmatic statements of fixed creeds, and saddles God's anointed ministers with executive burdens which sadly hamper them in the work to which they have been called. . . . Shall we not let God have His way in all things?

# 10

*Moving With God In New Dependence*

Ivan regarded the spacious Hornell property as an immediate necessity, but where were the finances? God miraculously provided for daily needs, but nothing had come in for the big project. With all earnestness, he endeavored to comply with the usual faith position, that of silence to others concerning the need—but still nothing came. Finally, in the January issue of the *Herald*, Ivan boldly presented a front-page picture and article on the Hornell property, under the title of "The Elim Bible School and Rest Home."

In this daring presentation of their need for the facility, he said, "Many of the Lord's people have spoken or written to us about their conviction that it is the Lord's will that we should acquire this property for the Bible School.

"For some time after the Lord had dealt with us personally about it, we trusted Him all alone, to supply funds for the purchase. Then, as He began to speak to others in various places, it was made plain to us that it is not an individual matter, but that it is the concern of the Body of Christ . . . so the Lord has spoken to us to place before His people the opportunity to give to this project, as the Spirit prompts. We believe that as those interested wait upon the Lord, the Spirit will indicate to each one what he or she is to do."

Responses poured in. There were criticisms—blame for advertising and thus leaning upon the arm of flesh. And there were promises—mostly to pray. But that was all. Ivan was learning patience, and it wasn't easy.

In the early months of spring, Ivan found another opportunity to express faith in God's guidance to relocate at Hornell. He plowed and planted in a field back of the sanatorium, to provide food for the coming camp meeting which should be held there, as well as for the winter needs of the school family.

Still no funds came in earmarked "Purchase of Property."

When April came, and commencement weekend, Elim hosted a record number of pastors and evangelists at a workers' conference, scheduled for that Friday. Response to the January appeal for funds had been negligible, and as Ivan looked the group over, his heart grew heavier. *Why?* Was there a reason, other than the present economic depression, for their lack of cooperation? It was with difficulty that he shrugged off his fear and thoughts of censure, and stood to announce the purpose of the meeting.

"Brethren, we have met today, in the leading of the Lord, to ascertain what God desires of us as a fellowship of people whose vision is the same—to see God restore to the Church that which has been lost through the centuries, and to move forward into all He has planned for His Church in this endtime. . . . There is a need in this present hour for the blessings of the Forward Move to spread throughout the Church worldwide. The fact that His hand is upon us, and the move of His Spirit among us, is witness to the fact that His purposes include us. We must not be remiss . . . shall we take time now to seek Him together, before taking up the items of business that face us."

Together they lifted their voices in praise; the Spirit moved in a prophetic flow as wave after wave of the presence and power of the Spirit washed over them. Ivan's fevered spirit relaxed, the anxiety of finances ebbing away in the flow of sweet fellowship. He continued leadership of the meeting, in which everything but the purchase of the property was discussed—increased zeal for missions, systematic giving to missions, and the recording of the distinctives of the Forward Move.*

Just before the close of the conference, a pastor referred to the widespread depression. Another earnestly declared, "God is rich; and since this depression is a judgment of God, why should not believers who are moving on in the will of God be exempt?"

"True!" Ivan agreed wholeheartedly, delighted with the young pastor's expression of faith. "Furthermore, I feel the school is proof of this. Why, this past year has been more prosperous than last year, even though the depression has worsened."

Then he stopped. What was he saying? Should he use the inspiration of the moment to challenge them to pledge their financial support for purchase of the Hornell property? Had God allowed this revelation of truth at this moment for this purpose? He looked about him in mute appeal.

But if the ministers recognized the implications of the truth just uttered, they showed no sign of it. The moment passed. Ivan felt constrained not to speak, so the matter never came up, and the day's conference closed. Perhaps God has another way to provide, Ivan thought. There were yet two days remaining of commencement services. He hurried away to a multitude of duties.

*Derived from the report printed in the *Herald* of April 1932: Based on the scriptural phrase, "the restitution of all things," the emphasized distinctives of the Forward Move were defined as follows: (1) A greater measure of the glory of God in evidence; (2) A stronger emphasis on divine healing; (3) Acknowledgment of visions, dreams, and prophecy; (4) Encouragement of a word of wisdom, word of knowledge, discerning of spirits; (5) Free manifestations of the Spirit, new to many; and (6) Dominion, or the authority of the believer in the spirit world.

But missions occupied center stage throughout commencement, and offerings were joyfully sent overseas. Pressed to announce camp meeting for that summer, Ivan stood before the congregation about to disperse, and with sinking heart declared, "Camp meeting will be held July 3-17—here at Red Creek."

Among the students participating in commencement exercises was a young woman who delivered her graduating address with fiery zeal, claimed her diploma, and then went forth to assist Mrs. Ella Moon in her church in Knoxville, Pennsylvania. Her name was Elizabeth Garate, and when she bade Carlton Spencer farewell, she wondered—would their friendship ever lead to marriage? She forced the question from her mind as she turned away. They had already discussed the termination of a close friendship, lest God's clear guidance be confused by a developing interest in each other. Elizabeth felt herself being drawn toward the mission field, while Carlton as yet had no such leading. He had spent long hours in prayer, often with fasting, endeavoring to be open to a call that would enable him to fulfill God's will, and qualify him to marry a girl with a missionary call. All to no avail. He had another year of school, and he hoped that by his graduation, the call would come. Until then, he must not endanger their obedience to God's highest and best for their lives. As he watched the lovely titian-haired girl hurry away from him that day, his heart sank, but he clung to his hope. He could wait.

On June 17, Carlton stood with Elizabeth, and others, before the altar of the Knoxville Pentecostal Church, their minds and hearts in a tumult of confusion and longing as they dared an occasional glance at one another over the kneeling figures of the bride and groom—Grace Moon and Cornelius de Groat. Grace had been a favorite at Elim, as a student and then as teacher of music. Cornelius was an Elim graduate who now pastored the assembly in Watertown, New York.

It was a lavishly beautiful wedding, the impressive appearance of Elizabeth and Carlton adding to the scene. But each was conscious that the other's cherished presence must be only a momentary blessing, that God must come first.

"Carlton, get a move on!" The voice was unusually sharp, and Carlton and his companion broke into a run, leaping into the back of the small truck just as Ivan threw it into gear. They looked at each other uneasily, swaying with the truck as it swung down the driveway and out through town.

Arriving at the woodlot, the boys jumped out with their axes. Ivan quickly turned the truck about and headed back to school without a word.

"Guess he's worried," Carlton muttered to the other as they turned to tackle the work that had been theirs for several days now. That week Ivan had resignedly announced, "We'll need firewood for next winter," and had appointed the two boys to the job—a hot one for the month of June.

Several hours later, the truck returned with Ivan, tightlipped and stern, behind the wheel.

They loaded the wood in silence, a big load topped by a long log that projected beyond the tailgate. Ivan climbed back into the truck, threw the gears into reverse to turn around, then stepped on the gas. He heard Carlton's scream, but failed to see that the projecting log was being rammed upward toward the rear window of the cab.

CRASH!

Carlton sickened as he saw the log go smashing through the window where his father's head had been.

The boys raced for the truck in terror. They found Ivan with blood gushing from a place near his temple—but alive. The log had barely missed crushing his head. Quickly, the boys pulled the log out of the way and rushed Ivan to town, where the gash was dressed and Ivan given to know that his escape from death was a close one.

From the moment of the crash, Ivan knew he could no longer go on planning to remain at Red Creek—God had given him marching orders, and it was up to him to place his feet in the Jordan and trust God to move.

That was the end of the hot, hard job of woodchopping for the boys. A few days later, pressed in his spirit to make some move toward obedience, Ivan set out for Binghamton to see the property owner. What he could do about the situation with no money for a down payment, he did not know, but he felt he should try to discuss it, at least. Carlton was with him, and on the way they stopped in to visit his brother Leslie at the home farm on Day Hollow Road.

"Whatever happened?" exclaimed Leslie in anxious concern as he noted the patch over Ivan's eye. After Ivan's explanation, and his interpretation of the accident, Leslie looked troubled. As they walked out toward the barn together, he looked about upon his fields and buildings. They represented a large investment of sweat and tears; and it was home to his growing family. But he knew his heart—and God. He dared not fight the decision any longer.

Clearing his throat, he ventured, "Look, Ivan, I don't know what this place is worth, but could it do for a down payment for you?"

Ivan was aghast. Could *this* be God's answer?

"But Leslie, this is your home! What about you and your family?"

Leslie shifted uneasily. "Lula and I have already talked it over. The Sanatorium's large enough for us, too, and I could help you with the work—that is, if you want us."

"Want you!" Ivan exclaimed, then choked on a lump in his throat as brother eyed brother in deep emotion. In a fervent gesture of mutual concern, they struck hands. Ivan's vision was now a shared one.

A quick trip into Binghamton and a consultation with the owner brought the signing of the contract, and the move began—Elim's third move in eight years.

Again, outdated trucks were enlisted for the job. Labor was volunteered, and the caravan began. Hilarious joy marked the ceaseless trips to and fro—a distance of some 100 miles. All available student help was enlisted for the cleaning job, and what a job it was! The scores of hospital beds with their crisp white spreads, over the three-years' vacancy had accumulated a black, oily film of soot from the railroad at the base of the hill. The same sooty film covered ceilings, walls, and floors, as well. There was no hot water, no electricity, no running water except from a faucet in the backyard—the students running it up the four flights of stairs, and working their way downward, room by room—a herculean task! Then came painting, a job which lasted far into the school year.

One of the most tireless workers was Ivan. Superintending the other workers, he bent his own back to many a task, adding the chores of clearing trees from the grove in back of the sanatorium to make room for the tent, setting up the tent for camp meeting, and getting in a dynamo to provide electricity for camp.

That camp meeting was a glorious one. Elim had "followed the cloud," and was tasting the sweetness of an obedient relationship with God. The Elmira newspaper carried this front-page report:

Tent Meetings Attract Many Worshippers

Pentecostalists Attract Crowds by Novel Worship—Devotion Is Paid by Individual Singing and Dancing Until Exhaustion Comes—Sexes Do Not Touch Each Other: *Hornell*—. . . . The tent meetings

100

have stolen all interest in all other things in this section. Every creed and denomination in the city; people from all walks of life . . . have poured into the tent meetings with the result that they have been accorded more consistent attendance than any religious meetings in the history of the city.

The magnet has been the form of worship. . . . Oblivious to the congregation . . . give vent to their worship by songs and solo dances. . . . Some, apparently exhausted, lay prone on the ground . . . never move a muscle for hours . . . range in age from 10 to 70 years and more . . . are jubilant and happy, and "have the power." . . . No affront has been offered . . . attendance from wide area, mostly rural folk . . . a predominance of the young, 18-19 years of age. . . . Frequently, when leaving each other for a period of time, the members kiss each other. . . . Motion pictures, dances, cards . . . banned.

So much for the outsider's viewpoint. From the inside, Elim and friends looked upon the occasion as a sacred celebration—as enthusiastic a dedication as God's people of long ago celebrated in the dedication of Solomon's Temple. Tent or Temple—what matter, when God is present? And as on that Bible occasion when God's glory moved in sovereignly, so that the priests could not stand to minister, so God took into His own hands the delightful task of dedicating Elim's new location.

It all happened suddenly, during the holy hush of an early service. And God didn't choose to use a revered guest speaker, or Ivan, or someone on staff, but a little-known woman in the congregation. Utterly lost in the Spirit, she moved into a poetic, acting prophecy that carried the congregation with her, marveling. Her words were of hallowing the grounds and buildings for God's purposes, of the place being God's gift to them, to be used for His glory. She moved about as she prophesied—to the altar, prophesying its blessings; outside around the grounds, sifting earth through her fingers as she moved; pointing to the buildings, all the time prophesying events that would take place in the facilities. It lasted for nearly an hour. When the time came the next day for the scheduled dedication ceremony, all acknowledged that God had Himself already dedicated His property—all they needed to do was worship, which they did with joyful abandon.

An enthusiastic participant in camp meeting activities was Elizabeth Garate, children's worker for the camp. In a smaller tent to one side of the grove, she daily conducted meetings for the children, assisted by other Elim students and graduates. God's glory among the oldsters in the large tent enveloped the children as well, so that their worship services were a joy to behold. Preschoolers joined older children in ecstatic worship that caused their faces to shine and their feet to dance. Often a spirit of conviction would rest upon them after listening to their Bible story, given in great fervency. At such time, there would be weeping around the altar. And among them moved the slight red-haired girl whose spirit flamed with zeal.

Carlton was equally absorbed in the essential chores of hosting so large a crowd, and in the personal dealings of God, whose awesome presence was molding his spirit for a larger sphere in life.

When camp ended, the two went their separate ways—Elizabeth to assist Elim graduates Reverend and Mrs. Robert Bressette in Ansonia, and Carlton to help with tent campaigns in other New York communities. Ivan followed up contacts for fellowship in midwestern states, extending the blessings of camp meeting through his rejuvenated ministry, and rejoicing in expanded horizons of fellowship.

That August, on the heels of the jubilant, crowded camp,

and in the midst of continuing cleanup and settling tasks, another daughter was born to Ivan and Minnie. Appropriately, they named her Faith—Faith Evelyn.

A prayer conference, held October 3 and 4, drew many pastors and workers to Elim to wait on the Lord. Significantly, the *Herald* reports that they discussed "the great need of a deeper, corporate prayer life, a real Spirit-filled ministry of intercession. The consensus of opinion was that rising up into the Spirit through praise and adoration of Jesus is the gateway to effectual intercession." Being released from the pressure of moving and settling, Ivan and the Elim fellowship were again ready to move into a fresh spiritual ministry.

The days that followed the opening of school were so busy that preparation for preaching and teaching was meager. But Ivan had learned the lesson of moment-by-moment communion with the Father, and his heart was continually prepared. So accustomed was he to blending action with worship that he could as easily speak in tongues in the barn as on the platform—and worship in the Spirit during a service while disciplining his child—or playing with him. He was as unassuming on the platform as in the field, and so unselfconscious that he quite lacked the pulpit dignity often expected of him.

To the outsider, such freehanded leadership might appear shallow and unconcerned, but not so. Ivan's whole life was a leadership role, Minnie sharing that role, and their consciousness of this did not allow for the familiar buddy-buddy rapport expected of the faculty-student relationship in schools of today. The stern disciplinary measures taken with the students were expressive of this same sense of responsibility, and who can say they were not necessary to Elim's total training purpose.

There were certainly times when censure was needed, even strict discipline that made a thunderbolt out of Ivan's usually placid personality. The twinkle would then turn to steel, and the form of discipline meted out would be minor compared to the awesome authority of his presence. But then would come the tears, genuine and conciliatory, with a warm embrace and kindly word of encouragement. There would always be prayer, too, and the principal and student would walk out of the office together, better friends than ever.

Though discipling, as a doctrinal theory, was not extensively projected in those days, the principle was there in practice. The revival firebrand, ignited during RBTS days, reproduced himself many times over in fulfillment of his calling, and it was a task that absorbed every moment and all his strength. Even his own family were incorporated into this passion for spreading revival. Each child, including the girls, was given to know that to preach the Gospel was the highest vocation he could wish for them. And he prayed to that end, fervently.

That year was Carlton's senior year, and a powerful molding influence in his life. From the hammer and chisel of such sculptors as Seeley D. Kinne and Max Wood Moorhead, the rough outlines of the man of God were emerging.

Guest ministries that year included James Salter of the Congo Evangelistic Mission; Joseph Wannenmacher of Milwaukee, Wisconsin, representing the Russian and Eastern European Mission; missionaries Hilda Longstreth and Edith Knoll; and pastor T. Arthur Lewis of Framingham, Massachusetts.

It was soon after this that Arthur Lewis joined the faculty, moving in with his family. He was a little man, called by the young people, "the laughing preacher," because of the delightful manner in which he operated in the Spirit during a service. He ministered revelatory truths—emphasizing redemption, the cross, and resurrection—with an impartation of life. His teaching brought a much-needed balance of Christ-centeredness into the classroom, and whetted the appetites of the spiritually-minded students for a deeper knowledge of Christ. However, for some students, the genius of his ministry was lost, and they at times would be more amused than blessed in his classes. At a later date, they would appreciate what they had unconsciously imbibed from his ministry.

About one young man student, Ivan often found himself wondering, "Will he ever make it?" He was a second-year student, outstanding in earnestness and missionary zeal, but he had a speech impediment due to a cleft palate that made communication a painful experience. However, Joseph Brown was sure that God had called him to Africa, and therefore was confident of God's enabling for that call. His pastor, Mary Danforth of Lyons, and Ivan, both sensed in the lad an unusual quality of spirit and devotion to the Lord, so they encouraged him in Bible school attendance, though with anxious reservations.

One day in Homiletics class, it came Joseph's turn to deliver a sermon. Hesitantly, Ivan called on him, loath to expose him to embarrassment.

Joseph walked slowly to the front, announced his text, then began to read, "The Spirit of the Lord is upon me, because He hath anointed me to preach the Gospel. . . . " He finished in a burst of sobs, intermingled with praising and adoration, arms upraised. The Spirit of the Lord then swept in upon the class so mightily that the entire group fell on their faces before God. No one present would ever forget that class and the witness of the Spirit to Joseph's call to service.

In after days in Egypt, still handicapped, Joseph saw the Spirit move in just such a sovereign manner, time after time, with many being saved and filled with the Spirit. From evangelism and pastoral work to administration of Bible schools and the famous Assiout Orphanage, the anointing enabled him to prove, "My strength is made perfect in weakness; therefore will I glory in mine infirmity, that the power of Christ may rest upon me."

To Ivan, the case was a beautiful confirmation to his own heart that the anointing of the Spirit is the prime requisite in ministry. Though God was sending to Elim many strongly talented young people, Ivan knew he must ever emphasize the all-importance of a Christ-like character and the Spirit's anointing.

Since these were depression years, Ivan and Leslie faced an impossible situation in operating such a large establishment and program. But that God honored their faith and hard work may be seen from the observation of a visiting Methodist evangelist, "This is the first place that I have been of late that there seems to be no depression. You seem wonderfully supplied in every way." The school year closed that April with all bills paid.

Joining the staff at this time was a young printer, Kenneth Dietze, who met Ivan on one of his early New York City trips. He took up the challenge of Elim's budding printing ministry with an enthusiasm born of a deep spiritual capacity and a longing to serve God with his skills. He assisted Ivan in making the *Elim Pentecostal Herald* a far-reaching and effective tool for revival in spite of financial and facility strictures. It was his vision and faith that through the years brought in the equipment necessary for Elim's expanding printing ministry. Ken also started the printing of tracts—often messages from camp meetings and conventions—which spread the message of Elim far and wide and, with the *Herald*, became a force for revival even on the mission field.

The *Herald* from the beginning was Elim's best, and only, advertising. Ivan also worked through the *Herald* to build the unity he so craved for the Body of Christ in its entirety. He well knew the power that the printed page could wield over the divided and lukewarm Church. He sought over the years to add the *Herald's* influence to that of other group periodicals who similarly sought revival. In a 1941 issue, when hunger for a Latter Rain revival was extant, but unity still an illusive dream, Ivan bared his heart in his editorial:

> One thing I want to emphasize to our readers . . . our message should have no uncertain sound. . . . Having correspondence with several writers recently, I find we have much teaching in common, but there are also minor points on which we do not agree. Doubtless these might be clarified if we could have prayerful consideration of each other's views, free from dogmatism and mental bias. *The most important of all is to have a unity of the Spirit. This must come before there is unity of the faith.* . . . I would like to submit a question to the leaders who see the "Latter Rain" imminent:
>
> "How far can we go in unifying our message so that it will have greater weight and effect?"
>
> Some of our teachings are doubtless traditional and we surely could lay them aside for the cause of Jesus Christ.

Along with the giving of his time and labor to the school, Ivan also personally shouldered a share of the financial needs. To start the pledges for the building of a tabernacle to house the next summer's camp meeting, he had pledged the first $1000. It seemed an awesome amount to Minnie, but she trusted Ivan to know the voice of God and obey it. A few months later, the $1000 came—a personal gift, but to Ivan it was clearly earmarked "tabernacle." He immediately began the excavation for its foundation.

# 11

*Gale Winds Blow Along The Watercourses*

Along with the triumphs and glory of those early years at Hornell, there were also confusions creeping into the Forward Move ranks. One source of confusion was a growing abuse of personal, directive prophecy, taking the form of marriage guidance or of missionary calls. Oh, the lies the devil will perpetrate under the name of the Lord! Because such prophecy was not exercised in public meetings where it could be recognized, dealt with, and teaching given to clear up misunderstanding, the practice grew, and confusions compounded. For example, there were occasions when missionary calls were induced to conform to such guidance in marriage, with the result that among some of the young people there came an unwholesome preoccupation with the very blessings God intended to use in their lives for His purposes. Caught in the snare of such prophecies, visions, and dreams, was Elizabeth, along with others.

Elizabeth by this time had moved to Mohawk, New York, to assist Pastor and Mrs. Norman Cook. Here she worked with another Elim graduate, Marjorie Preston, who later married Warren Denton, missionary to China and the Philippines.

They rejoiced with the pastor as they watched God move mightily among hungry denominational people. Fellowship was warm between the churches of the budding Elim fellowship, strengthened by the Elim student family who graduated and spread among the churches as pastors or assistants. Among these youthful workers, new developments in spiritual experience were enthusiastically shared, and occasionally became excesses in practice.

As an attractive and enthusiastic young lady preacher with missionary aspirations, Elizabeth gained the attention of a young pastor with a missionary call to a certain field. She resisted his attentions, still secretly holding to her first love, but the young man's persistence brought them together often. On one fateful occasion, a directive personal prophecy was given by a recognized leader, linking Elizabeth with him in missionary service.

When Elizabeth was told of it, she was thrown into utter confusion. She failed to recognize that all prophecy must be judged, and that directive prophecy must be accepted only as a confirmation of personal guidance already received. Tossing over and over in her mind the contradictory facts she faced, in an effort to sort it all out, she grew weary and fearful. There was the prophecy which pointed her one direction, but her heart led to another. Of course, many months had passed since she and Carlton had shared fellowship. How could she know he still cared? Had they not agreed to give each other up to the will of God, trusting Him to lead in their futures? And was not prophecy God's leading? How dare she refuse it? Finally, making the supreme sacrifice in her heart, she assayed to comply with the prophecy and the young man's desire for her. They became engaged, but she was not at peace.

One day, in an effort to strengthen her new dedication, she sat down to write a letter. "Dear Sister Spencer," she began, then stopped. This wasn't going to be easy, but she felt she must explain the upcoming wedding. There flashed back to her mind the prayer Minnie had made for her years ago, "Lord, if You wish Carlton and Elizabeth to be together, I know You will work it out for them."

With a groan, she again picked up her pen to write. The temptation to tell all was overwhelming—her questions regarding the prophecy, her revulsion for the planned wedding, her confusion over the missionary call, and her continuing love for Carlton. Bracing her strong will, disciplined over the past unhappy months, she found herself writing in a gay, brittle mood, "You probably have heard that I am soon to be married . . . and I really do love him!" Was it wrong to write a lie when it was necessary for doing God's will? After all, a wedding, and then going as a missionary, were exciting to anticipate, and, well, maybe she really did love him—hadn't she prayed to? If Carlton no longer cared, then surely she should forget. And besides, there was the prophecy—she had to love the one whom God had chosen.

Wanting desperately to do the right thing, she reread her letter, decided it must be the truth, and sealed it with stoic triumph—she had conquered her heart. But she was self-deceived.

The letter reached its destination, and Minnie was also deceived. Later, when Carlton's name began to be linked with another's, Minnie encouraged it, thinking that surely Elizabeth must know her own mind.

Finally, however, teaching began to come forth on the gifts of the Spirit, clearing the air of confusions. Camp meeting that summer majored less on physical manifestations and more on the disciplinary work of the Spirit. When the school year opened, with eighty students in attendance, Ivan shared his leadership responsibilities at the school with Arthur Lewis, so that he might circulate among the churches with a teaching ministry.

Then in November, 1933, there came the frightful, sobering experience of a tragic car accident involving Elim students, including Elizabeth and her fiance. For Ivan and Minnie, and the whole Elim family, it was a time of great heart-searching and grief, and came at a time of intense financial pressure as well. For Elizabeth, it was a time of desperate facing-up to the dictates of her own conscience, and a release from the fears of unwise counsel—prophecy so-called.

The crash victims had to be hospitalized and were at first placed in hospital beds crowded into one room. Two students, a freshman and a senior, were mortally injured. In the moments that followed regained consciousness, Elizabeth gazed at the young man in the bed next to hers, the man she had been planning to marry. It was all so plain to her now—her deception, then her self-deception. The fact that she was accountable to God, and not to another, regained its rightful priority in her thinking. Oh, how could she have been so fooled! Painfully, she managed to turn her back to him, and remained unresponsive to his attentions. In bitter tears of repentance, she wept her way back to the Father's heart, knowing it was His mercy that had brought her back.

Elizabeth came out of the hospital a bruised and battered girl, but with a wiser outlook on life, and free to live her own life in God. It was Carlton who was sent to bring them home from the hospital. Due to her neck injury, she had to ride in the front seat with Carlton, her fiance sitting in the back, but her physical agony precluded any conversation other than Carlton's kindly concern for her welfare. Since Elizabeth's mother had joined Elim's staff, Elim was Elizabeth's only home, so it was to Elim that Carlton brought her, along with her fiance.

In her convalescence over the months that followed, Elizabeth chose to ignore her past confusions, and slowly her health returned. As she grew stronger, she frequently accompanied Ivan and groups of students in their ministry among the churches. Often, she was pianist, and Carlton would be there with his trombone. They worked well together, and their ministries blended. She allowed herself to hope again, more sure than ever now that they were meant for each other. And she prayed—she knew how from long months of experience. Carlton, too, would know release.

From the time that Carlton had graduated in the spring of 1933, he had found an active place of ministry on Elim's staff, busy with many duties but also cooperating with Ivan and student groups and pastors in evangelizing throughout the area. In this capacity, he began to develop in vision and ministry, and shared with his father many school responsibilities. He thus learned early the sorrows as well as the joys that come to the man of God in a leadership position. He was also learning his need of a helpmeet who would be God's choice, not another's. When in the fall of 1934 a church was being started in Wellsboro, Pennsylvania, it was Carlton and Elizabeth who assisted Robert Bressette in the beginning weeks.

Springtime and commencement, and the proud moments when graduates received their diplomas. The last name had been called, the diploma claimed, and the class stood united in their mutual triumph—when suddenly the strains of a familiar tune broke over the congregation. In a matter of moments, the secret was out. Mendelssohn's Wedding March was replacing the recessional on the program. The reaction of the congregation ran the gamut from mild surprise to utter amazement. Among them, the oddly dignified but dearly loved teacher, Max Wood Moorhead, jerked to attention, with eyes and mouth wide open in consternation. He relaxed only when he recognized his favored former student, Elizabeth Garate, coming down the aisle in bridal attire,

*Ivan and Minnie on their wedding day, April 30, 1913*

*Endwell, 1924-1927*

*Ivan with his family before he left home—Ivan, front row center, with his mother and father, front right*

*Ivan and Minnie with the Elim staff of Endwell - L. to R., Mrs. Webster, Emma Womble, Pastor Mary Danforth, Ivan, Hazel Fairchild, Minnie, Lena Niles*

L. to R. *Ivan, T. Arthur Lewis, C.O. Dickinson, in the Hornell camp meeting grove.*

*The Ivan Spencer family [Paul in insert], 1948*

*Ivan and Minnie in the 1960's*

*The musical Spencer kids—summer of 1932*

*Elim students and faculty, 1931: L. to R., Minnie and Ivan;*
*Maida Blanchard and Max Wood Moorehead, editors of the*
Elim Pentecostal Herald; *Emma Womble, Dean of Woman.*
*Note: Carlton, a freshman, in third row, Elizabeth, a junior, in*
*fourth row.*

*First Lima camp meeting, 1952*

*Aerial view of Genesee Junior College campus*

*Hornell - 1932-1951*

*Red Creek - 1928-1932*

*Rochester - 1927-1928*

serenely beautiful and sure.

Awaiting her at the altar, face glowing in triumph, was the groom, Carlton Spencer. God had come first—and Elizabeth was his.

The April 1935 issue of the *Elim Pentecostal Herald* carried this simple account:

### Wedding Bells

Carlton Spencer, Class of '33, was united in marriage to Miss Elizabeth Garate, Class of '32, by the Rev. T. Arthur Lewis, assisted by the groom's father, Rev. Ivan Q. Spencer, and Mrs. Ella Moon of Knoxville, Pennsylvania; the double ring ceremony being used. The bride was prettily attired in a gown of white crepe with veil, and was attended by her brother Samuel Garate, of Rochester, New York. Her sister, Miss Edythe Garate, also of Rochester, acted as bridesmaid, and Alfred Reed of Endwell, New York, as best man.

Mr. and Mrs. Spencer are spending their honeymoon in Dansville, New York, where they are holding services.

In June, the newlyweds set off on a belated honeymoon to Florida—in company with dad and sister Mary! Since Ivan was preoccupied with his thoughts in preparation for preaching engagements, he drove straight through Washington, D.C., much to the dismay of the honeymooners. Even the anticipated visit to the capitol building was reduced to a receding glimpse from the rear window!

As a honeymoon, the trip was a frustration, but as an exploratory trip for fellowship and the possible establishment of a southern Elim, there was much success involved. This first contact with the South included churches in St.

Petersburg, Tampa, and Daytona Beach. Fellowship expanded warmly, and interest began to stir regarding a Bible school. The Elim party left for the north with invitations for a return trip ringing in their ears.

The camp meeting began with a flood, spiritually and literally. As the rains continued, the rivers overflowed, and local residents sought refuge on Elim's hilltop. For some, it became a double refuge as they sought and found the "Rock of Ages" at the tabernacle altar. The ministries of Reverend and Mrs. R.E. White of Tonawanda, New York, and Pastor George Hess of Chicago were a blessing, and prophecy flowed in unusual depth. The meetings were given over to the Spirit's leadership, "thus bringing forth a Body ministry . . . repeatedly shown by the Spirit to be God's highest plan for His Church in these last days." Liberty in worship with many physical manifestations still abounded, but a deepening influence came from an unexpected source.

Minnie was weary. Preparation for camp meeting, following so closely on the heels of commencement and the wedding, had taken its toll on her strength. One early morning, before camp meeting guests were astir, she slipped out of her apartment, down the back steps, and out into the cool, dim interior of the basement tabernacle. Sensing God's leading and presence, she made her way to the altar and knelt in expectancy.

She thought of the previous night's service—the shouts of praise, the rejoicing in song and dance, the excitement over what God was doing in their lives. Then she remembered the strange stirring in her heart of late regarding the Body of Christ. The more she had sought the Lord, the more her vision of the Church had expanded, and she sensed in a new way the potential of the Church universal—but also its shortcomings in the face of such potential.

An inward groan escaped her lips as her concern deepened into intercession. Suddenly she saw the Church in a vision as a literal body, but oh, so disjointed and sickly. There was even flesh missing from its right arm, and the elbow joint was stiff and inoperable. Then God began to speak to her in a most personal way.

*There must be travail to bring forth the members of the Body in unity, and with Christ formed in them,* He said, and it seemed He was actually taking her through an experience of childbirth—as physical as it was spiritual, and just as demanding in suffering. She cried out, "Oh Lord, You would not take people through this, would You?" Her eyes became fountains of tears. Her body, though exhausted, was divinely vitalized for the exercise of travail. She sensed she was but a representative of the whole Body of Christ that must struggle in suffering before bringing forth that people who would be without spot or wrinkle.

Minnie was aware that God had given her a revelation of a secret endtime ministry—one for which He had been preparing her, and one that would be shared by many others. When she arose to leave the tabernacle, she found her physical strength renewed, though she had given herself to an exhausting intercession. And there was an expectancy of spiritual blessing that belied the tears and groans of the experience—akin to the joy of a mother upon delivery of her babe. Oh, what a glorious secret ministry was hers!

She walked in the glow of revelation throughout the remainder of that hectic camp-meeting day. It was not until late evening, in the privacy of their bedroom, that she confided to Ivan her experience. Hesitantly she advanced the subject.

"Ivan, God has revealed something new to me, as—as personal as childbirth, and much like it in the spiritual realm."

The words sounded strangely in Ivan's ears, for not only was he too weary for further thought, but extremely happy with the victories of the night service just concluded. He tried to shift gears mentally to accommodate to his wife's strange mood. She seemed almost blue, and he couldn't understand it.

"What are you talking about," he asked rather impatiently, reminding her that intercession had always been her ministry.

"But this is different. I—I now know myself to be representative of the whole Body of Christ, in a travailing to bring forth a people who are united, and holy, and have God's power in the fullness Christ planned for His Bride."

Ivan watched Minnie as she spoke so earnestly, and with a new glow on her face. He was glad she had met the Lord afresh, though he realized he was not comprehending the meaning of her revelation. They were both tired, he decided, and needed rest more than anything else at the moment. He gave her a kiss, turned out the light, and tried to halt further conversation by saying, "Honey, you are tired. I wish you could have gotten in to the night service, you'd have been so encouraged. God is already doing a great thing in our midst and we need to be recognizing it and rejoicing!"

"But—but Ivan, I do rejoice in what God is doing; but we here are only such a small part of the Body of Christ, and even all this blessing is not God's best yet. How can we be content short of His best?" Minnie was roused now, and fighting the complacency she sensed in her leader husband.

But his sleepy reply was, "Pray on, Minnie; but some of us must do the rejoicing. God is moving in a great way, and I, for one, am glad!"

Minnie sank back in confusion. Why does fresh revelation have such a hard time gaining recognition in the Church, or could she be wrong? she wondered. But she ached for understanding, and went to sleep praying for others who would join her in this new secret-service phase of endtime ministry.

As Minnie shared in the services that followed, through

exhortation and prayer leadership, her revelation of soul travail as a Body ministry caught fire. Some of the morning services were given over to such intercession, and there came the balancing of celebration with surrender to God's deeper and broader purposes. But her depth of travail, with its unusual manifestations of deep groans and cries, was not understood by all, nor appreciated by some whose joyous celebrating of personal blessings precluded all concern for the needs of the Church universal.

In the months that followed, Minnie sought to accommodate her ministry to the more generally accepted spirit of rejoicing. Often at an altar service, when travail would come upon her, she would try to stifle her cries, even stuffing a hankie in her mouth to remain silent and unnoticed. But her body suffered from the lack of that divine vitality that had at first been hers when she had abandoned herself to the Spirit.

One night God gave her a dream. She was in a river, out so far that she had to swim. Not being a swimmer, she made for shore, only to find herself entangled with the weeds and slime of the shallows. She was forced to return to midstream, where she was conscious of divine life flowing through her body. She awoke with the knowledge that her physical well-being depended upon her continuance in the ministry of travailing prayer.

Asked by a friend, "How did you come into this ministry?" Minnie responded, "I didn't. It came into me . . . it works life in me . . . brings enlargement to my being. I am naturally hard, and I had to be broken. This breaks me. This is meeting my need, and I don't have to worry about myself. I am a part of the Body, and the prayer affects me as it does any other member. . . . The Lord may have to lay hold of a few of us and cause us to suffer. Anything, only that He can fulfill that which is on His heart in these days . . . in His Body, the world over."

In time, there were others whom God similarly

anointed.With Minnie, they formed an intercessory team, undergirding the ongoing ministry of Elim, but reaching even farther by faith to release the anticipated showers of latter rain upon the needy Body of Christ. An oft-repeated Scripture was, "Ask ye of the Lord rain in the time of the latter rain "(Zech. 10:1).

That October found Leslie and his family moved to the Red Creek facility to be caretakers and to oversee the simple schedule of services and ministry of the rest home. Carlton and Elizabeth were pastoring the church at Endwell, New York, and Ivan spent his time in the school, working the farm, and following up new contacts for fellowship.

Elim sustained a great loss when Max Wood Moorhead died in the spring of 1937, after seven years of faithful service as *Elim Pentecostal Herald* editor and Bible teacher. The influence of this unusual and devout Englishman was deep and lasting. His love for the mystics, and the projection of their words and lives through the pages of the *Herald* characterized the man to all who knew him. Another outstanding characteristic of this spiritual giant was his dauntless faith in the utmost meaning of truths set forth by Elim, going father than most in his acceptance of the oft-preached doctrine of victory over death.

Ivan's endorsement of this doctrine, which seemed violated by its advocate's death, is a classic example of his affirmation of truth as he saw it, even when under fire. Pressed by the clamoring of unbelievers, he published the following statement in the May issue of the *Herald:*

Some may question, "Why did Brother Moorhead die if he believed in " 'victory over death'?" Allow us to also ask, "Why do people get sick and die who believe in Divine Healing?" A Bible truth is not changed because it is not always experimental. Sometimes there are reasons from man's side and sometimes it is from God's point of view. God is sovereign and can always do as He chooses. While in prayer for Brother Moorhead's recovery, God spoke to one of our company and said, "If I want him up higher, what is that to thee?"

The restoration of the Church to its bloodbought privileges is by stages. . . . In the very last days of this dispensation some will come into their bloodbought privilege of translation and victory over death. As yet they have not come into that realm, but shall soon do so. Brother Moorhead embraced this vision.

As the winter wore on, financial pressures increased. The mortgage principal awaited liquidation, while the small offerings only nibbled away at the interest. Ivan's dream of operating a farm-school, with the business of farming to pay off the mortgage and operational expenses, came back into focus. He increased his farming, using the students as help, one by-product being valuable work training for them.

Then, very gradually, month after month, and chronically, year after year, Ivan's priority on spiritual ministry slipped. The school classes and chapel services often suffered from his absence. If he wondered at the wisdom of leaving the word of God to serve tables, he no doubt firmly believed it to be only an emergency measure to take care of indebtedness. Surely God was not pleased to have the mortgage continue unpaid, he reasoned.

Perhaps, too, Ivan's performance of farm duties as a sacrament—the milking stool had always been his best prayer spot—preserved his own spirit from coldness, though the overall effect upon the school was a cooling off in spiritual fervency. In his busyness, he was not aware, as was Minnie, of deterioration in blessing. So the little body of intercessors labored on under new pressures of need.

Meanwhile, another trip south had netted an invitation to

establish a southern Elim, connected with John Knizely's church in Mobile, Alabama. Ivan sent Carlton and Elizabeth down to administrate it, and teach, being assisted by Reverend and Mrs. Ralph Thompson of St. Petersburg, Florida. Later, Kenneth and Helen Bennett, recent Elim graduates, joined them on staff. Ivan and Minnie's family now numbered eight children, their last, a daughter, Bernice Fern, being born in March 1937.

The southern school was in its second year when a letter came from Ivan telling of his dire need for help at the home base. Leslie had been recalled from Red Creek, desperately ill. Moorhead's death had left a void that had not been filled. There were also dissatisfactions among some of the younger ministers of the fellowship. So Carlton and Elizabeth, with their firstborn, David Carlton, returned to Elim. To the care-worn grandparents, Ivan and Minnie, cuddling their first grandchild and dedicating him to the Lord was a thrill indeed!

With the addition of Carlton to the staff, Ivan decided that conditions were advantageous for an expanded farm program, to more quickly liquidate the mortgage monster. He called Carlton into his apartment one evening to lay out his plans.

"I'll rent more farmland to the south and over by the cemetery. We'll plant more potatoes, which will be a good seller this fall."

"B—but, dad," Carlton broke in, "I didn't come back to enable you to do more farming. You're supposed to be freed to get on with your ministry here in the school and among the churches. . . . They—they need you, dad!" His voice was pleading, and Ivan wavered for a moment. Was he doing the right thing? Was the mortgage all this important? But, yes, it had to be paid. Their indebtedness must not continue.

"Look, Carlton, I know what I'm doing. This mortgage has got to be cleared away before I can be free to give myself unreservedly to the ministry again. And this is the only way I know."

Minnie had been sitting by, quietly mending, but as she listened, her anxiety deepened. She knew what God had been saying to her in her intercessions for Elim. This further step into farming was out of line, she was sure. She watched Ivan as he outlined his plans, so determined and sure of himself. How could he be? She had to interrupt.

"Ivan, your spiritual ministry comes first—have you forgotten?"

Extending calloused hands, now trembling, Ivan declared passionately, "God has given me hands that can farm, and I must follow this as His leading for my answer. I've tried every way I know to get the money, even trying to sell houselots off the campus, but nothing works. I—I can make this work if I have more land—and more help. You've got to help me, Carlton."

Carlton relented, aware as he did so that he was joining his father under a crushing load that neither of them could carry without God's help. But was God really in this? He knew the fellowship ministers would not think so.

# 12

*Fellowship Ranks Thinning—Revival Fires Continue*

When Carlton returned to Elim in 1938, enrollment was still high but showed some decrease. With the start of the war, it dropped more rapidly. Since Elim was not recognized by the government as a ministerial training school, the young people of the Elim fellowship faced being drafted if they attended Elim for ministerial training.

Carlton had been home only a few months when Elim lost a great friend in the passing of Ella Moon, pastor in Knoxville, Pennsylvania. The camp meeting that followed soon after the funeral pointed up how deeply the loss was felt by the camp congregation, with whom she had been a favorite speaker for so many years.

Then, in April of 1939, the day before Easter, Leslie Spencer was laid to rest. This was a blow to Ivan personally, but also for all of Elim, because of his sacrificial service and godly influence. He was only forty-one years of age, and it was an especially sad and confusing time for his wife Lula and her five young children.

A phrase in Ivan's account of his death in the *Herald* expresses the tender respect with which he held this loyal younger brother—"his associations were always sweet." From the faith Leslie had reposed in his brother's vision and ministry, Ivan had gained a partner and a commitment that made the Hornell location possible—he could not forget that. The same *Herald* account closes with Ivan's poignant plea, "Would not God be pleased to remove the mortgage in the near future as a memorial to our beloved brother?"

To facilitate cooperation among the churches, and perhaps to help rally the dispirited pastors, an expansion of the original association was developed, with Ivan Spencer as General Chairman, T. Arthur Lewis as General Secretary, and Thomas Griffith as Missions Secretary and Treasurer. A missions committee included evangelist-pastor C.O. Dickinson and Charles Denton, an Elim graduate of '35 and a pastor. With this, area fellowship activities increased. Sectional monthly fellowship meetings developed, and later a youth thrust, under the leadership of Bernard Hinman, Elim graduate of '36.

Ivan's participation in these decisions of development was in one sense a concession to the desires of the younger ministers of the fellowship, whose aspirations were high for their growing churches.

Then Elim suffered the loss of a valued teacher and spiritual leader when T. Arthur Lewis moved away to take a pastorate. Also, Seeley D. Kinne, the aging seer whose vivid prophetic ministry had thrilled many a camp meeting congregation and stirred Elim churches to a deeper spiritual ministry, moved permanently to California. When Thomas Griffith resigned shortly after, Carlton fell heir to the dual responsibility of secretary to the Fellowship and Missions—this added to an already full schedule of teaching and pastoral duties. Fortunately, Elim at this time gained the assistance of Ruth Shippey, a returned missionary—one of the Ethiopian Trio—who served temporarily as office manager and worked enthusiastically with the missions outreach.

With the war came economic crises to the nation, and to Elim, so that Ivan's financial concerns deepened. He saw no way out but more farming, which meant more hours away from the school and ministry among the churches. His dilemma seemed complete, and he was tormented with a growing sense of failure. There was his failure to communicate to the pastors that vision and motivation which impelled his own ministry; his failure in coping with the multiplying facets of fellowship activities; his distaste for desk work which produced those haunting stacks of unfinished business; and now his inability to keep up with spiraling operational costs.

Pressures—pressures—and nerves tensed like catgut on a guitar, tighter and tighter. To the farm and the milking stool, to the hoe and turning sods of mother earth— Ah, there is rest, relaxation, healing! So Ivan retreated yet more, his physical labors being the safety valve for a developing nervous heart condition.

Meanwhile, dissatisfactions increased among the fellowship ministers, in spite of their organizational advances. All about them, other Pentecostal organizations were prospering, numerically and materially, and it was easy to compare and become discouraged. Perhaps they faced the same temptation the Israelites fell into when they clamored for a king like the other nations. But certainly in their weakness, they needed the close guidance of their spiritual leader, and it was for this reason that a representative group of them arrived one spring day at their headquarters office at Elim.

They found the President, their General Chairman, to be out. Nor was he busy in a class, nor among the churches. A messenger was sent to bring him in—from the farm.

In those moments of coming, Ivan's discouragement

deepened with embarrassment, and the futility of his situation caused him to draw even more into his shell. As the men carefully, but thoroughly, presented their case, Ivan only listened, already knowing their feelings. Most of them were his sons in the Gospel, and there was a mutual love and respect that made the confrontation all the more painful. But why didn't they understand his position?

". . . So you see, Brother Spencer, we really need you. Your presence and counsel at these times of tension could save us from making mistakes that hurt our churches, and the fellowship. If—if you'd only free yourself from all this farming business so you could lead us . . . " The voice trailed off in pleading tones, and in the silence that followed, Ivan cleared his throat to speak.

"I—I want to help—but with all these responsibilities what can I do?" He paused a moment, then asked pointedly, "I wonder if any of you would change places with me—assume the responsibility of keeping the school supplied and functioning?" His eyes searched the group, challenging them. When there was no response, he closed the issue with the cryptic announcement, "Since there is no one, I'll just get back to my farming." He turned and left the office, to work out his frustrations with his hoe—and before the Lord in prayer. The pastors returned to their churches—and problems.

Sharing these frustrations, Carlton traveled as secretary among the churches, seeking to inspire fellowship meetings and projecting the cause of missions. The results were increased giving and more missionaries sent to the fields. When Sixto and Ruth Lopez, Elim graduates, were led into the field of Cuba, Carlton and other Elim associates made exploratory trips into the Island. This paved the way for more Elim graduates—the Peter Sedas, the George Veaches, the Paul Andersons, and others—to serve there. Their vital witness over the years, until Castro's occupation, is still reflected in the national church.

Meanwhile, Merritt had graduated from Bible school and joined Arthur Dodzweit, a former student of 1935, in pastoring and evangelism in New England. Mary was serving on the faculty, blessing the school with her anointed ministry in music and acting as confidante to Ivan in many problematic areas. Eva worked in needy areas of New York and Pennsylvania. Often using the students as assistants, she pioneered Sunday schools and churches, and assisted with youth work. Surely Ivan was proud of his family, and grateful for their valuable contribution to his, and Elim's, ministry.

In an effort to more adequately supply the demands of the school budget, Ivan proceeded to buy a farm in the neighboring town of Burns. With this acquisition added to his rented farmland, he laid his plans for intensive dairying, and the market-gardening of those staples bringing the greatest returns, squash being a major item.

That July of 1942, the camp meeting was glorious beyond many others, with amazing manifestations and expressions of Body ministry that promised imminent reality for the Latter Rain revival so long and earnestly sought. Many of the young ministers were refreshed and encouraged to believe God for the revival that would solve all problems. The next issues of the *Herald* carried their printed convictions, with stirring challenges to press on, and reject the arm of flesh that could rob them of God's best.

Added to the cohesive effect of the camp meeting were the encouraging letters of an increasing number of Elim youth, including Merritt Spencer, who had been drafted into the Armed Forces, and their pleas for the united prayers of the fellowship.

That fall, Ivan's well-laid plans for school provision suffered utter defeat. The market prices dropped to a ridiculous low—squash bringing only two cents a pound! It seemed that God had blown upon his plans like so many ashes. And if Ivan was desperate, so was Carlton. He understood his dad's longing to ease the financial pressures— it was a load on him, too. But he also bore the load of the continuing discontent of fellowship ministers who felt neglected by their leader, and who poured into his ears their misunderstanding of homebase operations.

In May of 1943, the constitutional meeting of the newly forming National Association of Evangelicals was convened in Chicago, and Ivan was among the 500 delegates present. He returned home thrilled.

"It was truly wonderful, Minnie, to hear those denominational preachers praying for the outpouring of the Spirit," he enthused. Minnie was glad to note the new hopefulness in her husband's attitude.

"There were fifty of us Pentecostal representatives present," he continued, "and it seemed incredible that we could have the privilege of fellowship and conference over business matters with those who have ostracized us for years."

Minnie listened with absorption. Her intercessions for revival for the whole Body of Christ gave her an intense interest in what he was saying. She thrilled with him when he declared, "You know, Minnie, I believe it is an indication that the latter rain is very near—when God shall bring us all into the unity of the Spirit."

That summer, Ivan attempted another full-scale farming program, but the crops turned out poorly, providing less than usual of the produce needed for the winter's food supply for school and for camp meeting demands. Though gas rationing had affected camp attendance, and their camp ads in the *Herald* now had to include "Bring your own sugar," Ivan still retained the policy of "Meals on the Freewill Offering Plan." Later, he had to add, "Please bring potatoes and other vegetables, canned or fresh, as these are in scant supply here."

Carlton's position as Fellowship secretary brought him some painful experiences during these years. On one of his customary trips among the churches, he dropped in one Sunday morning on an assembly that he had had a part in pioneering some years earlier. As he slipped into the back seat, awaiting recognition from the pastor, he noted with thankfulness the increased attendance and some familiar faces. Then began a pleasant reminiscence, including the young pastor who at this moment was doing an excellent job at song leading. Carlton had been involved in his conversion some years before, and he'd since graduated from Elim—was, in fact, one of their most promising young pastors. But there had been signs of disinterest lately that had brought concern.

The service progressed with seemingly no recognition of Carlton's presence. When the meeting closed, and the congregation had filed out after shaking hands with their pastor at the door, Carlton was chilled at the embarrassed announcement of his friend and fellow minister.

"Carlton, I now hold credentials with another organization, so it is best that you not come to the church anymore, though of course you are welcome at my home anytime."

That next spring, Ivan acted upon an increased conviction in his heart. His confrontation with the ministers in his office had been a traumatic one. And though he had shown no signs of change at that time, heart-searching had ensued, and a relenting in his spirit toward their desires. This was indicated in his action of selling the Burns farm property to Leslie's widow and her family. Her oldest son, Andrew, was a senior in high school and capable of assuming farm responsibilities due largely to the excellent training he received while working for his uncle at the school. Little did Ivan dream that, in later years, that very farm under Andy's management would pour literally tons of food yearly into

Elim's larder.

But Ivan had no intention of relinquishing the farmland adjoining the campus. Had he not always farmed to supplement the school's food supply, and was it not good training for the students who helped him? Then also, farming had been a loved and familiar life since childhood. It had become a refuge from the pressures that threatened his health. Could it be that he had forgotten the admonition he so often gave his Bible school students—"When fingers cling, they sorrow bring"?

That fall, Ivan visited in a distant city to get a much-needed rest. Typically, he again sought new contacts with Pentecostal brethren, and he was dismayed as one after another hastily produced their credentials to let him know their affiliation. Several boasted of their headquarters locations—from California across the nation, including even Elim! Then there were others who boasted, "We have no headquarters—we are independent." Ivan was also appalled at the kind of advertising used in promoting revival campaigns.

He returned to Elim grieved in spirit and in the next ministerial meeting described his experience. "I am concerned to think that anyone might be following Elim rather than God, and in so doing miss His best. I've been praying, 'Oh God, let me see the headship of Jesus, and that my "headquarters" are in heaven'—will you pray this with me?"

He continued by adding, "After watching all this fleshly activity among those Pentecostal preachers, and considering the whole carnal structure that produced it, I felt like asking God to dynamite the whole thing—to blow it to destruction by the dynamics of the Spirit—and over the rubbish raise up the standard of love, holiness, and power, by the coming of the mighty latter rain! Oh, the crying need of a broken spirit in God's ministers. Let this be our prayer—'Break, break, break me, oh Lord!' "

The ministers sat with bowed heads as Ivan concluded his challenge. Could it be that God was also blowing upon the ashes of *their* organization? Wasn't it really the dynamics of the Spirit that they needed in their churches, rather than this strengthening of organizational structure?

But one by one, the well-trained fledglings of earlier years, now established in proven and respected ministries, began to drop out of the ministers' conferences and the camp meetings. God richly blessed in the services—often through outside ministries, though not always—and there were yet healings, baptisms, conversions, and Body ministry. But as a progressive, purposeful movement, Elim was in retrenchment—from the head down.

No one deplored this more than Ivan. Caught in a financial vise, he suffered in silence and worked as one possessed—driven to nibble away at the mountain that was God-sized! And as he farmed, he prayed. Oh, where was the God of that prophet-farmer Amos?

It was during these lean farming-for-finances years that Ivan produced some of his best written work for the *Herald*. Long hours of milk-stool praying netted the man of God an inner enlargement and a mellowing of his spirit for a wider, yet more mature fellowship in future days. Nor was it coincidental that at this time Pentecostal denominational representatives were found attending Elim's camp meetings.

Some of these men observed an expression of worship and vision unknown to their own ranks and beyond their ken. One organization official was heard to say, "That Ivan Spencer and his group are right—they have tremendous truth—but they are premature, way ahead of their times." Perhaps he was speaking of their emphasis on Brideship, a select group from out of the Church who alone would attain the purity Christ seeks for in His Bride. This linked with the emphasis that had been made over the years on "selective rapture" and the "Manchild Company"—those who attain to such complete identification with Christ and the Cross as to become immune to the working of death in either spirit or body, also called victory over death. This latter doctrine had received more emphasis earlier, through its principal advocates, Seeley D. Kinne, Ella Moon, C.O. Dickinson, Max Wood Moorhead, T. Arthur Lewis, and a guest pastor from New England, James Hicks. Now that most of these had passed off the scene, the teaching had settled into a wholesome reminder of the potential power of the Cross in the believer's life.

These were astounding declarations, to be sure, but there was a basic truth common to all—that holiness and power go hand-in-hand in the plan of God for His people. Certainly such truth as this, stripped of unnecessary complications of detail, is desirable. But, admittedly, complications were developing in the area of selectivity. And Ivan's vision of worldwide revival was losing perspective.

Shut up as he was by circumstances, and pained by ministerial differences, Ivan had over the years become introverted in his vision of Churchwide holiness and power. This now caused him to see the Bride as a select *few* rather than *many*, the world over. When world conditions seemed to indicate Christ's imminent return, missions projects would dim before the necessity of "the preparation of the Bride" for translation.

So it was that often in missionary services, so announced, Carlton and Ruth Shippey would have to move, and move fast, to preserve the focus on missions, and to balance out deeper life with evangelism outreach.

Then there were some Pentecostal leaders looking in on Elim during these years who liked what they felt, but not what they saw—sometimes. "Excesses," they called them— those unusual physical manifestations that often would accompany a prophecy, or an anointed sermon. A joyous victory march is disturbing to an onlooker whose thirsty spirit whispers, "March!" but whose starchy anatomy says, "Nothing doing!"

Now Ivan was well aware of extravagances in worship, but he had learned his lesson well at Red Creek—God's fledglings require leeway for learning the ways of the Spirit. Too, revival was a passion with Ivan—he *must not* quench the Spirit and lose out on revival, at any cost! It wasn't easy for him to sit on the platform and allow an exuberant member of the Body a harmless Highland fling, when in the congregation, a fellow Pentecostal leader sat watching, aghast and annoyed.

Nor was Ivan beyond embarrassment when those of the "mixed multitude"—always on hand where there are free meals and freehanded services—would begin to operate in the flesh. At such times, God would balance Ivan's leniency with the gift of government, perhaps bringing into play the gift of wisdom, knowledge, or discernment.

On one occasion, it was anointed elbow grease that served the purpose. A man who had persisted in speaking out unwisely in the service received Ivan's orders from the pulpit to take his seat. He did, but soon bounced up again. In that moment, two ministers shot off the platform, apprehended him in the middle of his absurd speech, and carried him out bodily. It was done quickly, and with finesse. After all, where the Spirit flows freely, the wheels can mesh quickly and quietly—cushioned in "Oil"!

Another so-called extreme for which Elim was criticized in these days, and even more so earlier, was the practice of putting out a chair for one who wanted to receive the word of wisdom for his need—which word would be forthcoming from the group of ministers gathered prayerfully about him. From the beginning of this Spirit-inspired practice, during those glorious revival days at Red Creek, the Lord had used this form of personal ministry to strengthen and empower the members of His Body. Often the word of wisdom or liberating prophecy came in this manner, and often it was Ivan whom God used. But Ivan did not confine his wisdom ministry to the chair practice. How sad that some fell into the trap of requiring the ritual before being receptive to God-given counsel. Others made the mistake of accepting every word uttered at such a time as God-given wisdom, infallible.

Perhaps the Church has yet to learn that no amount of horizontal relationship—member to member in the Body— can replace the personal vertical relationship—member to his Head, Christ—no matter how valid the ministry. Our loving Creator God is jealous over that intimate "Voice" communion with His own.

But some of the Pentecostal leaders who visited Elim during the late forties found a quality of spiritual expectancy and openness that corresponded with theirs. It was with these that fellowship was pursued. Ivan planned with them for leadership gatherings, for prayer and preparation of heart for the coming Latter Rain revival. These gatherings were to be held in various headquarters locations—Georgia, Michigan, Canada, Hornell, and Providence, Rhode Island.

So, in spite of financial pressures and misunderstandings, Ivan kept his spirit in vital contact with God. His zeal sought and found new horizons of influence for revival. During these years of search for fellowship, he traveled north, south, east, and west in his voracious hunger for latter rain blessings—so earnestly sought also by Minnie and the little group of intercessors. At such times, out from under the crunch of home-base demands, Ivan could relax and receive the refreshment his spirit craved. Especially was this true among the Spanish churches of New York City. "Saint John" they called him, as he poured out anointed ministry and love upon them in response to their warmhearted fellowship.

Not all contacts were so satisfying, however. On one visit in a remote state, all started out well with sweet oneness of purpose, when suddenly a prophetess arose to prophesy who it was that should be the speaker of the service, and even what he should preach. Amazing, thought Ivan, as the service progressed in that direction. But then the same thing happened in the next service, and the next. Ivan went away grieved, and wiser for his visit. The godly leader had lacked discernment and authority, and a bad situation was worsening, tearing down the good thing that God had started. Ivan returned to Elim with new appreciation for the gift of government that Christ has placed in His Church.

A later contact with that group revealed that the "elite" among them had retreated to another area to await rapture as the Bride, while the others at home worked to support the needs of those awaiting their rapture. Eventually the whole work went into dissolution, with financial and spiritual shipwrecks as grim reminders of the necessity of the headship of Christ in the operation of His Body. Some of these sincere but deceived saints were later salvaged into other churches and now serve the Lord wisely and well.

Elim, as an oasis in time of drought, over the years has been greatly indebted to many outside ministries—camp meeting speakers with anointed preaching and deliverance ministries. Among these, in the late thirties, were Elton Davis of Florida, and John Knizely of Alabama, whose healing ministries were outstanding, and later, the British-educated young Indian mystic, Lam Jeevaratnam, of Gudivada, India, with a singular ministry in the casting out of demons.

Then there was the gentle-spirited J. Rufus Moseley, author of *Manifest Victory* and *Perfect Everything*. He added the fragrance of his ministry on union with Christ. He was an early advocate of the way of love, since championed by the Jesus Movement. He was also an extremist on health foods, which apparently made him an authority on the subject for one woman who asked, "Reverend, will I go to heaven if I eat pork?" His unhesitating answer was, "By all means, and the more you eat, the faster you'll get there!"

That he was a buoyant, joyous person is reflected in this excerpt from the *Herald:* "If we give Jesus and His love to all—all the time—we will abide in Him all the time. If we do this, we will have so much Heaven going to Heaven, that the going will be almost as good as the arriving!"

Rufus Moseley shared with Ivan that vision of the Church that was beyond their time. The fact that his books are now being reprinted in paperback proves the timelessness of the open fellowship and love relationship advocated by him some thirty years ago.

The year of 1945 found the youth work of the fellowship flourishing, with their own camp program and monthly rallies. The missions program was on the move, sending eight more missionaries that year, including Arthur Dodzweit and "Bud" Sickler, and their wives.

A business meeting was held in May 1947 to begin legal incorporation "for a more systematic cooperation between the leaders and churches of this Fellowship." Significantly, Ivan called for a day of prayer to "seek the perfect will of God for us as a body at this time."

In a later issue of the *Herald* he commented, "Many have been the efforts to bring forth greater accord and more harmony, such as organization and other natural methods to encourage cooperation and fellowship. Generally these have not accomplished the purpose for which they were planned *because some spiritual principles have not been fully recognized*—the most important of which is the *headship of Christ.*"

The camp meeting of 1945 was a red-letter date in Elim's history, for God graciously moved upon the hearts of the people—mainly through the members of the Elim Former Students Association—to give in cash and pledges the total amount of the mortgage. It was a day of jubilee for Ivan and Minnie—and Carlton—but it did not come as a surprise to

Ivan. God had shown him in prayer one day that He would kindle the hearts of former students to supply the need. At long last, rest came into Ivan's heart on the issue that had tried him so long.

April, 1946—just forty years after April, 1906, the beginning of the mighty Azusa Street visitation in Los Angeles, which had ushered in the Pentecostal movement. The awakening had then come as answered prayer for many earnestly praying groups of Christians across the nation. Probably no one appreciated his Pentecostal heritage more than did Elim's loved Bible-swinging, devil-routing evangelist—C.O. Dickinson. Though his ministry lacked polish, it scintillated with the power of God, and many were the healings and conversions that took place in his limited sphere of operation in the northeast. He was also known for giving the word of wisdom, or knowledge, in times of counsel on knotty problems.

But though not widely known, he was broad in his vision, and keenly aware of Church and world needs. His big heart bled with those of other intercessors over the creeping coldness and impotence of the Church. He gave himself as wholeheartedly to prayer as to preaching, his wife joining him in intercession. When this April, 1946 rolled around, his heart was ripe and ready to see a repeat performance of Azusa Street. The Easter weekend fellowship meeting seemed the perfect time for it to happen.

Ivan and Carlton were seated with others on a filled platform when C.O. Dickinson arrived and took a chair at the side of the church. As the service progressed, he waited in an agony of expectancy, tensed for that heavenly visitation that would sweep through the room and emancipate them with a freedom such as they had never known. It just had to come—but it didn't.

Before ever the benediction could be uttered, he thrust himself heavily to his feet, and cried, "Oh God, it is time for

Thee to work. Oh God—" Any further utterance was choked with great, shaking sobs. Such heartrending fervency stunned the congregation and ministers—and dismayed them. They well knew that this man's prayers were a force to be reckoned with. In the face of his selfless sobbing, they were smitten with the coldness of their own hearts. It was perhaps the best sermon on prayer that C.O. Dickinson ever preached, and perhaps the last, for from that time on his heart and body weakened, and within the year, he was laid to rest—a prayer-warrior who yet speaketh, and whose intercessions in only a matter of months were to be gloriously answered with latter rain. To Ivan, this loss in the ranks was a staggering one, but the memory of that Easter fellowship day, and the sobbing hulk of a man pouring out his life for revival, remained to stimulate his own intercessions.

Other losses by death came during these years: Mary Hastie of Avoca, Pennsylvania, and Mary Danforth of Lyons, New York; both pastors and veteran faith warriors. At the latter's funeral, an impressive number of missionaries were present—most of them former Elim students—whose ministries began under her spiritual guidance. To Ivan and Minnie, both these deaths were keenly felt personal losses.

The camp meeting following that memorable Easter of 1946, witnessed the burning of the mortgage in a special service that brought much rejoicing and further offerings for building repairs and improvements. Also during that camp meeting, the fellowship leaders met daily, and after much prayer and consideration followed the Lord's leading in appointing seven men "recognized by all to be set in the Elim work by God . . . that those in these offices be freed from other activities to do the work to which God has called them." For Ivan, this meant release to move among the churches, with help from Ward Lusk in school duties.

The years of pressures had taken their toll, but burdens were beginning to lift.

# 13

*Latter Rain Revival And Expanded Ministry*

Taking the release afforded him by a lightened financial load, Ivan headed south with Roy Hill, just returned from Africa after a ten-year stint of pioneering in back country Kenya. It was a pleasurable trip for Ivan, with Roy's good humor and enthusiasm for missions rubbing off on him refreshingly. Then, while in West Virginia ministering in a camp meeting, he took note of a ruddy-faced youth who exhibited a singular interest in the services. Always on the lookout for student material, he engaged him in conversation, with the upshot that George Veach arrived at Elim that fall to enroll as a student.

George was only seventeen, a farm boy, but he had already attended part of a year at a Holiness Bible school. He had left there because he had been led into the Baptism of the Spirit by a Pentecostal roommate, and was thereafter dissatisfied with the school. Since Ivan needed help with the farm work, it was only natural that George would become his right-hand man in off-study hours, in the barn and in the garden.

Elim opened with an enrollment of twenty-six that year,

attendance still being greatly affected by war, as well as the continuing criticisms leveled at the beleaguered fellowship from outside and from within.

A new challenge came Ivan's way that winter, in the form of a wayward teenage daughter. His heart was often filled with concern for her, and the need became a part of his milking-stool prayertime. One late afternoon, as streams of foaming milk were filling his bucket, Ivan was deep in thought. As his hands worked, his thoughts became an agony of prayer. Oblivious of George's nearness, he cried aloud his petition.

"Oh Lord," he pled brokenly, "we have not raised Faith to serve the devil, so I ask now that either You will save her, or that You will take her. I refuse to have a child of mine serve the devil!"

George, who was milking further down the line, heard the cry and was chilled at the implications of the prayer. It was made with such force and conviction that he knew Faith was in trouble.

Faith had often used George as a confidant for her escapades. Though she had given her heart to the Lord that summer during camp meeting, under Mattie Howard's ministry, she had succumbed to the desires of the old crowd at school that fall.

When George found her, he spilled into her ears the prayer he had heard, and his fears that it would be answered to her hurt. Faith stood trembling, eyes brimming, and a weight of guilt settling upon her rebellious spirit. Now what would she do? she wondered, knowing well the power of her father's prayers.

"Won't you go to him and confess what you're doing," George pleaded, "and get right with God?"

It wasn't easy, but she was already finding that the way of the transgressor is hard, as well, and in the light of such a prayer, there was nothing else to do. So it was that Ivan and

Minnie were finally taken into her confidence, and with tears of repentance, and forgiveness, Faith came back to her Lord—to stay.

For Ivan, the work scholarship of farming was a serious training experience for his students. When he worked with the student in farm work, he therefore expected implicit obedience, and always got it—well, usually. It seems that George, with his prior knowledge of farming and equipment repair, at times felt he knew better than Ivan what to do. One day, on a matter of machinery repair, he dared to stick to his point.

"But that's not the right way to do it," George insisted to Ivan, heating up over the matter. "It should be fixed this way," and he proceeded to explain his method, angering Ivan with his stubbornness.

"We will fix it this way, George, " Ivan said firmly, explaining his way again, and refusing to budge in his decision. Just then the dinner bell sounded across the fields, and Ivan arose, stiffly announced, "Dinnertime," and strode off toward the school in cold silence. George, in turn, was so angry, he refused to follow and remained in the barn until after the meal was over.

That evening during the service, as Ivan was preaching, George came under great conviction for his lack of submission to this father in the faith. As the sermon progressed, George grew more miserable and repentant. Finally, when Ivan concluded his sermon, George jumped to his feet.

"I—I've got to say something—"

Ivan interrupted him. "Just a minute. You were angry at me today, weren't you?"

George was embarrassed, hurt. "Y—yes, sir, and I'm very sorry. I want you to forgive me, and I want you all to pray for me that the Lord will deliver me from this hot temper."

There, it was out—and with it the sobs would come. He

heard Ivan asking others to join in, and they gathered about him in compassionate prayer. Then George could hardly believe his ears— What was Ivan saying?

"Now I was angry at you also today, George, and I want you to lay hands on me, and pray for me."

Today the vice-chairman of the Elim Fellowship, George says, "It was the most humbling experience I've ever had."

That January of 1948, during a week of prayer at Elim, the Pentecostal Prayer Fellowship was formed, in order to facilitate the convening of an increasing number of interested Pentecostal leaders. Carlton was named secretary of the prayer fellowship, and as such kept in close touch with them all. Included were the International Pentecostal Assemblies, Pentecostal Church of Christ, Zion Evangelistic Fellowship, and Elim.

It was just one more indication of a growing expectancy of revival, and as preparation, a desire for unity. Ivan and Carlton were both stirred to new hope, not only for Elim, but also for the Pentecostal movement as a whole. These fires of expectancy were fueled by Ivan's contacts with the National Association of Evangelicals and the pending development of a continental Pentecostal organization, and by Carlton's contacts throughout the west and in New England.

As the spring progressed, George grew interested in Ruth Spencer, and it became obvious—to one person at least. With Elim's social rules being what they were, such an undercover activity as love palpitations in the disciplined hearts of Elim students required a Sherlock Holmes to detect. But the elderly Sister Dillenbeck did. Being a spiritual mother with commendable concern, she straightway went to George.

"George, I found you talking with Ruth Spencer today. This is against freshman rules. Furthermore, you know it isn't Christian to sneak talks with her. You should ask permission for it."

George gulped, and acquiesced. He sought out Ivan whom

he had learned to both fear and love. When the principal was father of your sweetheart, what could you do?

"I'd like to ask permission to talk with Ruth this Sunday afternoon," he ventured, face red and heart pounding.

"Very well," said Ivan, "fifteen minutes, then," and he continued with his work.

That Sunday afternoon the fifteen minutes—so short—stretched into thirty-five minutes, and George afterward began to feel guilty about taking advantage of the permission granted.

The next day, as he worked in the barn with Ivan, he took the opportunity to say, "I have an apology to make—" Then he hesitated. "Well, what is it?" asked Ivan, and George continued with reddening face, "You gave me fifteen minutes to talk with Ruth, and I took thirty-five minutes." Ivan's reply was simple. "Oh, I see." And that was it.

When a week later George went to him for a similar permission, Ivan said briskly, "Well, let's see. You took thirty-five minutes last week, didn't you? As I recall, you were supposed to take only fifteen minutes. So it looks to me like you better forget it for the rest of the year." And that was it!

A few weeks later, Ruth graduated, and Ivan's gift to his daughter was characteristic of the man—a book, on the subject of the Finney revivals. But though Ruth might have squealed with delight over a wristwatch, a string of pearls, or some other usual graduation gift, she nevertheless cherished the book. Any gift at all was an unusual expression from her father, and a book would certainly declare his fondness for her, since his most cherished posessions were his books, especially those on revival. So the pretty blond daughter, whom he had taught to consider preaching as the highest possible calling in life, did not disdain his choice, though perhaps Ivan would not have noticed if she had.

Commencement was past; already it was late June, and

there was much to do before camp meeting in July. Carlton was alone in the office one afternoon when the door opened to admit two men. One was his younger brother, Paul, now twenty-five years of age but sustaining a nervous disorder that would place him among that group today called "special." And *special* Paul was, for he dearly loved the Lord, was always cheerful, and outstanding in his faithfulness about the school—whether it be washing tins, peeling potatoes, or picking up around the grounds. He was Minnie's right-hand man, and dearly loved by them all. But he had a stranger in tow, and Carlton had to find out what Paul had in mind.

After greetings, and explanations, Carlton turned to Paul. "Are you sure you want this insurance? It will cost you two dollars each month, you know." Paul nodded his understanding of the agreement and, with some further deliberation, the life insurance policy became his.

They left the office, and Carlton went back to his work, wondering somewhat at Paul's interest in an insurance policy. Merritt had just returned from the Service, and this same agent had sold him a policy, but Paul—well, he was a money hoarder, and perhaps it was well that he take on this small responsibility.

Carlton turned back to his desk with a sigh. The work was piled up from his month away in the west, and from his father's absence to get the planting done. And now Ivan was attending the National Association of Evangelicals Convention in Chicago. Carlton smiled as he thought of his dad's mixed feelings in going—his natural impatience with organizational machinery, then his eagerness to see if that machinery were headed in the right direction—revival. And this convention was to be followed by a gathering of Pentecostal leaders to consider the possibility of closer cooperation and fellowship. This last had decided Ivan on leaving his farm work to go to Chicago. His appetite for

Pentecostal fellowship had been whetted by the prayer gatherings that he and Carlton had already been convening with leaders of other small Pentecostal groups. He mustn't miss anything God might be doing.

Since Ivan's travels seemed to focus on fields afar, rather than among the fellowship churches, another appointment had been made that fall of '48. Arthur Stanton, Elim graduate of '35 and a man of proven spiritual ministry, was called to join Elim's staff as fieldworker. Carlton accompanied him on some of his early trips including New England. His ministry of faith emphasis became a great blessing and encouragement during the crucial months of continued waiting for the Latter Rain revival, now so generally expected.

Ivan returned from Chicago just in time to get the camp meeting underway. It was a forceful one, with many strong preaching ministries, including that of Thomas L. Osborn, now a world-famous evangelist. His sermon on "The Creative Word" set the keynote for the meetings. Missionary emphases were provided by George Upton, Missions Secretary of the Pentecostal Assemblies of Canada, and M.S. Shoucair of Lebanon. Attendance represented twenty states and Canada, Cuba, Puerto Rico, and India.

Then Ivan was off to the second exploratory conference of Pentecostal leaders, held also in Chicago, August 3-4. He had been back home only three days when tragedy struck his family.

Paul had accompanied cousin Andy to Mary (Spencer) Reed's home in Schenectady for a visit. On their way home, the car had skidded, wrapped around a tree, and snuffed out the life of young Paul. There was no doubt as to Paul's readiness for death, but it was truly a heartbreak for all concerned. There was some redemption for the heartbreak, however, when the double indemnity clause of his recently purchased insurance policy provided ample funds for a much-needed boys' school in Africa. Construction began immediately, and the school was dedicated "In Memory of Paul Spencer."

Minnie sorrowed over Paul's sudden death as only the mother of a "special" child can. The closeness of such a relationship, and Paul's loyal faithfulness which kept him at her side, only increased the pain of his absence.

Ivan, numbed with his grief, sought out his hoe the morning of the funeral. Remorse filled his heart, and great sobs shook him as he hoed his way across the field. It was thus that Arthur Stanton found him, not long before the funeral was to begin. He was in charge of the services and was concerned over Ivan's absence.

As the young minister stood there beside him, compassion in his very presence, Ivan gave vent to his thoughts.

"I—I should have done more for Paul to make him happy. I could have bought him a bicycle—he would have enjoyed that. Oh, why didn't I do more for Paul!"

The young minister stood in silence before this burst of grief. What does one say to the "might have beens" of life? But surely it was the word of wisdom that came to Arthur Stanton that day, to bless and heal a father's wound.

"You gave to Paul the most important things—faith in God and a happy Christian life. You taught him to pray. You led him into the Spirit-filled experience, and he learned to delight in worship. You led him by your example in these things—and he was happy with these gifts."

But perhaps Ivan did need a lesson on concern for his family's happiness, for the rigid standard he set for his own dedication to the will of God often involved his family in sacrifices not always voluntary on their part. One example was his lack of interest in Christmas giving, though sometimes at the last minute, he would indulge thoughtlessly in such tricks as gift-wrapping a potato or piece of coal for the tree that Minnie would decorate to cheer the school apartment for the holiday. Vacations were somberly quiet with the students home for Christmas, and Minnie empathized with the children's need for a jolly, festive occasion.

The children learned to be suspicious of these gifts from their father, and to steel their hearts against disappointment. They could always count on simple gifts from their mother, however, and so could the students who had to remain at school and therefore were invited to join the family on Christmas day. Minnie expected no gift from her husband, and received none. But then, she had none to give him either, for money was always scarce. She chose to share his standard of dedication, and was happy in the sharing. Although she was not without disappointment from the lack of the finer things she still loved, she did not blame Ivan. She knew he could not understand such longings. But he did understand her beautifully in her spiritual desires, and with this, she generally contented herself.

That summer of '48, Carlton, Edward Hill of the Zion Evangelistic Fellowship and some new missionaries traveled to Cuba and stayed for a few weeks of tent evangelism with the Elim staff on the field. Many were saved, healed, filled with the Spirit, and Elim's missionary work in Cuba received new impetus. Already the Sixto Lopezes were engaged in successful radio ministry and had plans underway for a church to be built in the city of Matanzas. Elizabeth's mother, Ina Garate, was working in one of the village churches, assisted by the Wilhelm sisters. Now the Peter Sedas had joined the field staff.

Meanwhile, Ivan attended the founding meeting of the new Pentecostal Fellowship of North America, and was named to its Board of Administration.

That December of 1948, Ivan and Carlton traveled to the Zion Evangelistic Fellowship in Providence, for the scheduled Pentecostal Prayer Fellowship gathering—never dreaming that in their purpose for meeting, faith would soon become sight.

They were deep into prayer when a member of their group, arriving late, entered the room and ventured to share what he had heard of a visitation in Detroit. When later the brethren broke up their prayertime to return home, there was excitement and expectation among them. Ivan stopped off at Elim only long enough to confide the event to Minnie and take her along with him to Detroit where, just possibly, their long-awaited latter rain was falling.

Carlton then called the returning students to prayer, suspending all classes for the imperative of heart preparation for the coming revival. In high expectancy, they awaited news from Detroit, while humbling their hearts before the Lord. Carlton took time out for a hurried editorial for the *Herald* in his father's absence, to communicate their excitement of faith to their readers:

> We hear of visitation in many cities. . . . These reports confirm the conviction in our hearts that 1949 will witness a glorious heaven-sent visitation. . . . The Spirit-born efforts toward closer cooperation and fellowship among Pentecostal bodies is, we believe, further evidence of this. God is breaking down barriers that would hinder the tide of this flow of the Spirit, so that hungry hearts everywhere may receive. It is true that not all will receive this promised visitation, but the Lord is so working that organizational barriers will not hinder the hungry. We at Elim are suspending classes and are uniting in prayer for the promised visitation. Let us unite in prayer.

Meanwhile, Ivan and Minnie had arrived in Detroit and were soon ushered into the basement sanctuary of Bethesda Temple. As they became aware of the hundreds of people on their faces crying out to God in humiliation and brokenness, they knew that God was in the place. Says Minnie, "The Scripture, 'Break up your fallow ground,' was being enacted before our eyes." They, too, fell on their faces, and the Spirit wrought a work in their hearts that was new, and made them new.

In those days spent in the Temple, with little thought of meals and mundane duties, they witnessed marvelous depths of spiritual victory—manifest in conversions, baptisms, healings, deliverances, and impartations of gifts and ministries by the laying on of hands. Holy spontaneity replaced special programs, though there was much teaching. Prayer groups met as early as five in the morning, continuing into the afternoon. And it was easy to pray—one wanted to do nothing else.

According to Sixto Lopez, who visited Detroit at this time, this spirit of prayer was "characterized by brokenness, yieldedness, illumination upon the Word, restfulness in His presence, loss of appetite for food, and a flow of love and fellowship that made total strangers feel 'at home' with one another. There was an inward bubbling of joy, yet also a great solemnity; there was a liberating freedom yet a sense of the burning fire of God sanctifying the thought life. Also, through the laying on of hands, there was confirmation of missionary calls, and the setting apart of individuals for specific ministry. In such an atmosphere, all lukewarmness disappears. A key phrase seemed to be, 'a mighty going down before the Lord.' "

Minnie prefaced her report of their visit with this significant bit of verse:

In this hour of visitation
When God's hand is pressing hard,
Shaking, shrinking and expanding,
I'll not fear—Thy love will guard.

She continued, "Surely we need to recognize the hour of our visitation. . . . Our hearts are encouraged in the vision

God gave us so many years ago. How often we reminded ourselves of the Scripture, 'Though the vision tarry, wait for it. . . .' Bless God, I believe the waiting days are over, and we have entered into the endtime revival. We must now believe for the fullness of Joel 2:23."

Yes, revival had come, beginning in North America with Canada, then moving down the west coast to as far as Los Angeles. Across the country it came as a great tornado, touching down in many cities, but especially making Detroit its focal point. Why? For Minnie, it was exciting to hear Mrs. M.D. Beall, pastor of the Temple, describe their revival prayers and radio programming over the past seven years. Why, it was seven years ago that God had laid upon Minnie the ministry of travail for revival! Her heart leaped within her as she sensed she was hearing the cries of the newborn babe, now delivered.

When Ivan and Minnie returned home, they found the Elim family in a similar spirit of prayer. God continued His gracious moving, and Ivan extended an invitation for those outside to "come partake of the 'feast' of revival." That February issue of the *Herald*, which carried remarkable articles on latter rain experience and teaching, sold out and had to be reprinted.

Carlton's first question when his dad returned, was sparked by an obviously *new* Ivan.

"What's new in it, dad? Some new doctrine, or procedure—or what?"

Ivan's answer was a searching look, and the suggestion, "Go find out for yourself, son."

So Carlton and Elizabeth, with Eva, Sixto, and two staff members, drove out. They capitulated, as did Ivan and Minnie, before the force of conviction and repentance that held them all in God's presence, and under the searchlight of Calvary. Ministering in apostolic authority were Winston Nunes, Paul Stutzman (both became close Elim friends and trustees), Elmer Frink (who later became a teacher at Elim), Stanley Frodsham (who became a close Elim associate), Mrs. Beall, and her son, Jim. For Carlton, his visit in Detroit was a new beginning in God, with fresh motivation, clearer vision, and a broken, tenderized spirit, befitting the man of God's choosing for Elim's leadership.

Coming into Elim that spring to drink of latter rain blessings were thirsty pastors of the Elim fellowship, and returning Elim missionaries from many parts including strife-torn China. What an oasis was their alma mater for these former Elim students!

Revival among the students was so profound that one, George Veach, who now pastored a small country church, asked Ivan if he might leave school for fulltime evangelism. Ivan remembered his own request in RBTS days, and Mrs. Baker's wise counsel. But he also remembered his frustrations in trying to get started in the ministry after his marriage and first-year settling down at farmwork in Spencerport.

"It is my wish, George, that a student fulfill the prescribed three years. However, Christ is the Lord of the harvest. Whatever He says to you, do it."

George prayed more, then left. And God did graciously send revival to his little assembly. Later that year, he married Ruth Spencer, and still later, they went to Cuba as missionaries, and thence to Argentina.

Prayer had continued through the balance of the school year, commencement convention marking a turning of the tide for Elim. Paul Stutzman was the principal speaker for the convention, and ministered in true apostolic anointing. The convention was so blessed that it lasted a week longer than scheduled, ending in a high tide that bespoke richer blessings to come.

That May, the *Herald* carried an editorial by Carlton: "Visitation is spreading . . . throughout the west . . . in Detroit. We are trusting the Lord to establish centers farther east, and are preparing our hearts before the Lord . . . for a gracious visitation in the coming camp meeting."

That was the camp meeting "outstanding in unity . . . in going down before God in humility and weeping. Deliverances followed confessions, and longstanding bondages . . . were broken." Some among the hungry crowds that thronged the humble basement tabernacle, were disappointed—they had seen more spectacular and miraculous things happen in previous years at Elim. But those attuned to the Spirit humbled themselves in God's presence—and the mercy drops of latter rain would fall.

W.I. Nunes was used of God in laying the foundation by his teaching ministry throughout the camp.

A visitor of note at that camp meeting was Fred Poole, father to John Poole now of Philadelphia, an apostle from Great Britain's Apostolic Church. He and his wife soon found their way to the altar with cries from their hearts for latter rain refreshing. In a service following, the camp Bible teacher, Winston Nunes, with Fred Poole, Paul Stutzman, and T. Arthur Lewis laid hands on Ivan and Minnie, setting him apart for apostleship and travel among the churches, across the nation and overseas. This was in confirmation to what God had been speaking in the depths of Ivan's heart, and Minnie's, concerning an expanded ministry to the whole Body of Christ.

To be set apart for apostolic ministry was not a new thing for Ivan. In early Forward Move days, Seeley D. Kinne, with other brethren, had ministered to him by the laying on of hands, naming him to apostleship. But what is an apostle? And why is the recognition of such a ministry important today?

Even in the early thirties, there was a reticence among Christians to use the New Testament term "apostle," perhaps based on a fear that no one in the twentieth century could approach the standard set by the apostle Paul. But that

Christ "gave to the church some apostles" is beyond doubt a promise for the whole Church age, as are the other named gifts and ministries. So then, the ministry of apostleship must be resident today in the Body of Christ.

According to scriptural definition and example, an apostle is one who is sent by God, the very word meaning "sent one." In the spirit of humility, he wields authority in the affairs of the churches, church government being one expression of this. He is a church planter, and as a father, carries the spiritual burden and oversight of those churches birthed by him. His church-planting ministry is accompanied by enabling supernatural power, wisdom, knowledge, and prophetic expression. His burden of all the churches is constant, and he manifests a willingness to suffer for their sakes. He is a man of sterling and transparent character, ever holding an uncompromising standard of holiness before the ministers who labor with him. His vision encompasses the whole Body of Christ, worldwide.

Ivan, in concluding his *Herald* article on the subject, wrote: "Though we may not see men today to compare with Paul, we do need to recognize apostolic *ministry*. Let us honor Jesus by recognizing His ascension gift ministries."

Since quality of character, essential to a man in such authority and leadership, calls for extreme maturing processes, it is little wonder that Ivan's spiritual growth came the hard way—blow upon blow, aimed at every avenue of his being and ministry. As wine is matured and produced in finest quality by being poured from vessel to vessel, so God's men are subjected to the vicissitudes of human experience until they are indeed sweet to the King's taste.

During that same week of camp meeting, Carlton and Elizabeth were called forth, and with the laying on of hands (a scriptural practice being restored to the Church) were set apart for the leadership of the school. According to the prophecy given Carlton, "The mantle of your father is upon you, enabling you for the task."

Ivan's editorial that New Year of 1949 referred to a Scripture befitting this moment in his—and Elim's—history:

The Bride "cometh up *out of the wilderness, leaning* upon her Beloved."

But even as bright clouds of latter rain burst upon the waiting Bride, there were angry clouds of opposition forming in ranks along the horizon—and advancing threateningly.

# 14

*The High Cost Of Revival*

Those heart-searching days of deliverance in Detroit had stirred a bubbling of hope in Ivan. Perhaps he would yet be part of the endtime revival ministry that would usher in Christ's coming and kingdom. How he had longed for this ever since his early Bible school days!

But there had been so many frustrations—his failure in his first pastorate, the door closed to India, the rejection of loved fellow ministers, the lonely path of faith and dependence upon the Spirit's leadership in all things—then the crushing financial load that had seemed to be squeezing the life out of him, both physically and spiritually, so that even his own ministers had lost confidence in him. How could God ever use him as he had hoped to be used? He was bone-weary, and he sensed bitterly that "hope deferred maketh the heart sick."

Then came Detroit, and latter rain at last! And since then, confirmations that set his soul atingle. Nothing would surprise him now. Had not God reminded him that He would use broken things? The *Herald* had carried this reminder:

Christ is building His kingdom with earth's broken

things. Men want only the strong, the successful, the victorious, the unbroken, in building their temples. But God is the God of the unsuccessful, of those who have failed. There is no bruised reed that Christ cannot take and restore to glorious blessedness. . . . It is when a beautiful grain of corn is broken up in the earth by *death* that its inner heart sprouts forth and bears hundreds of other grains. And thus on and on, through all history, all vegetation, all spiritual life, God must have *broken things.*

So Ivan sought the Lord in humble expectation, and laid his plans. And of course, Minnie was there at his side. His release was hers, too. With the care of Paul now in the Lord's hands, there was only Bernice to plan for, and she could go with them.

After an excited farewell, they were off, and Minnie's emancipation matched Ivan's. How they praised and prayed as they traveled over the highways, and faith rose higher with every mile. God had spoken, and sent them forth.

Thus began that part of Ivan's ministry for which he is best loved and known—an apostle of love to the Church worldwide. In a day when travel was only for the wealthy, the merchant and the idle, such missionary trips as became Ivan's ministry were indeed a miracle.

Into the south and throughout the west they went. South Carolina and Florida, in special services that witnessed God's power at work through their ministries; in Mobile, Alabama, with Pastor Milton Ennis; then to Beaumont, Texas, with Pastor Harry Hodge and his large fellowship of churches. Here in a convention, the latter rain was falling in a glorious way, with the huge tabernacle filled to overflowing nightly. Ivan wrote of the pastor, of other anointed brethren, and of meetings as "flowing in real Texas style—how easily we could flow with the sweet spirit that was manifest. We were made to feel we were one of them!"

With a nudge from the Lord to move on, they reluctantly farewelled Texas and visited in St. Louis. There was opposition here to the Latter Rain revival, but Ivan rejoiced in the forward march of the two assemblies and the growing fellowship. His ministry among them was heartily received, and their fellowship deepened. Then there was a tent revival in Indiana, a stopover for precious revival fellowship in Ohio, and home again. It was an exhausting trip physically, but stimulating in spirit.

But what would have been the apostle Ivan's message to these churches on his first missionary journey?

Where there were criticisms of the revival, for abuses of prophecy and doctrine, Ivan drew lessons from the past:

Those of our day who oppose speaking in tongues and prophecy use the Irvingite movement as an argument against them, because of misleadings resulting from prophetic ministry among them. . . . But we as Pentecostals heartily endorse these gifts they brought to the forefront, though we do not endorse some of their doctrines. . . . Why should we not appreciate the pioneers of our day in the things of God, and if they make mistakes, profit by their experiences—gathering out the precious and leaving the rest? The virtues of the Spirit are ever manifest in any fresh move of God—this is the test of whether a move is of God or not. This present outpouring of the Spirit has these virtues in a marked way.*

Where there was an overweening loyalty to denomination that threatened acceptance of revival, Ivan would give his testimony:

---

*The quotations for Ivan's trips are excerpts from articles written by him during and after the time of his visits among these churches, no doubt expressing the convictions he voiced at this time.

Some years ago, in studying the Pauline epistles, I caught a vision of what the New Testament Church really consists and functions, under the control of the Holy Spirit. . . . I have sought earnestly the New Testament order, endeavoring to depend upon divine leadership, but not in an independent spirit. In the early Church the order was simple, and it is difficult for those trained in organization to see it. When "the Lord added daily to the Church . . . " to what were they being added? Not to a denomination, but to Jesus Christ.

Men of God's calling and spiritual endowment were God's gift to the Church. . . . Jesus said, "I have ordained you." . . . The gifts of wisdom, knowledge and prophecy were theirs in the government of the Church. God has never recalled these gifts. . . . The Church is still in the process of being "fitly framed together" and must still have the same divine equipment as in the early days. Human organization tends to limit the Spirit's guidance, to circumscribe truth, to destroy the oneness of Christ with sectarian coldness.

But beware of the tendency, in turning away from human system, to go to another extreme—independence and lack of submission. This also will bring discord in the Body. . . . God will bless the people who recognize Spirit-anointed leadership and apostolic authority. There was in the New Testament Church a recognition of the leadership by apostles—fathers in the Church.

Where there were wounded spirits from opposition to revival, and confusing doubts had set in, Ivan would build faith with such words as these:

God has "hidden these things from the wise and prudent and revealed them unto babes." It has ever been so. . . . What does it mean to be "wise and prudent"? To be full of reasoning, over-cautious in acceptance of truth and light. The simplicity of life in the Spirit and in the ways of God . . . only a revelation of the Spirit can bring to the human heart. The heart must have a childlike attitude—an artless, open, unassuming nature, with faith for the impossible. God has hidden many precious truths in His Word, veiled to the natural man, that he might believe from his heart, and not from natural reasonings. God's challenge to us today is to believe Him, and accept the fresh revelation He is giving in His Word.

And for those in whom he glimpsed an uncharitable attitude toward their brethren within the revival movement, Ivan drew from his years of farming that homely illustrative material that hits the mark:

Unless a grain of wheat falls to the ground and dies it "abideth alone." . . . Here is the gate to all spiritual progress. Death must come to the flesh, our own ways and struggles, and what we are by nature . . . letting Jesus live out His life in us. . . . Nor can we raise a crop with such insects as caterpillars and locusts devouring them. There are insects in spiritual life also, such as pride, self-righteousness and unbelief . . . . The bias of sectarianism—whether denominational or undenominational—is our problem. It is this 'ism' in our hearts that divides the Body. . . . In these days when God has risen to "shake everything that can be shaken," some undesirable things are coming to the surface in our lives. . . . We need to "let brotherly love continue" (Heb. 12:27-13:1).

In summing up his trip, Ivan's admonition to the Elim staff family on returning home was, "May we all continue to move on with God, for we have yet only seen the beginnings of latter rain. Let us not mistake the work of preparation for the fullness of the promise." Ivan was fast expanding to fill his niche in God's plan.

In days of prayer preceding the Fall Convention that year, a student reported receiving a vision of Christ standing atop the tabernacle, beckoning in all directions with outstretched arms—"Come!" And truly the people did come, from all directions and in overflowing numbers. They came with hungry hearts from across the nation and even from overseas, and Christ captivated their attention. One spoke of this revival as being a "Not I, but Christ" revival—and certainly this was borne out by the exaltation of Jesus in every ministry and service. There was also a strong emphasis on I Corinthians 13—Love—and a new theme—"The Christian Home,—Divine Order in the Home."

This convention also marked the beginning of Psalm-singing as we know it today, through the ministry of a blind sister on Elim's staff—Rita Kelligan. This gift developed over succeeding months and years, giving us the rich heritage that forms part of the charismatic renewal worship today.

School opened with enrollment doubled, and Carlton welcomed the return of T. Arthur Lewis as teacher, and Chester Gretz, a Houghton College graduate and close friend of Elim for some years, as Dean of Men and teacher. Gretz would later serve for years as Elim's vice-president, and today is an Elim missionary to eastern Europe.

During the January week of prayer, Ivan taught revival truths to the whole student body and guests assembled, using the typology of the tabernacle of the Old Testament. Assisting in worship and fellowship were James and Phyllis Spiers. The week lengthened into three weeks when the Spiers remained to minister among the students with their richly anointed ministry in song and the Word. The Spirit moved among the students and revealed the hidden things of dishonesty through the ministry of discernment, and there were many deliverances. The Spiers continued in ministry among the Elim churches, and eventually started a church in the city of Buffalo.

Fathering the churches of his own fellowship again became Ivan's delight—and when he met a need for correction, he humbly gave it, rejoicing in the ready acceptance given his advice. The breaches were healing. If he found some whose rejoicing in latter rain blessing had become a source of pride, he would warn:

If any who have come into this present spiritual awakening feel that the latter rain is exclusively theirs—they are not clear on the Spirit's emphasis at this time—that is, the oneness of the Body of Christ, regardless of organizational affiliation. Who are the "custodians of God's visitations"? No group can singly lay claim to anything that comes from God. It rightfully belongs to the whole Body of Christ!

And where he found contention over doctrine, with a reluctance to enter into revival because of the mixed multitude included, Ivan counseled,

It is possible to be so dogmatically orthodox that we miss what God is doing. . . . The Lord is primarily concerned about the attitude of our hearts. If He can deliver us from our self-will and critical spirits, He can surely straighten out our doctrines. . . . If we don't wake up to what God is doing, many of our denominational brethren will come into latter rain, while we who have thought we had it, but who have been self-satisfied, may be left behind!

A letter from David du Plessis at this time encouraged both

Ivan and Carlton, who were earnestly desiring that God would send revival among the schools of the nation. David was at that time an instructor at Lee College in Tennessee. He wrote, "A glorious revival has broken out. In a Sunday evening service, while the congregation sang, the Spirit settled down upon the group and filled the place with a strange but glorious presence. Tongues and interpretation followed and the people streamed to the altar . . . a glorious prayermeeting . . . many souls were saved and others filled with the blessed Holy Spirit. The meetings continued for over a week, with deep heartsearchings, confessions and humiliations. Students went to their teachers, and teachers to their students, to make restitution and remove hindrances. The visitation is still on!"

That winter also Ivan visited a Bible school in Maine. He found open acceptance for his ministry, and resultant rain from heaven blessed both school and churches of the area.

Elim's Spring Commencement Convention drew overflow crowds again—with hunger for God. Thirteen hundred pressed into the modest basement tabernacle. Attendance was augmented by the presence and ministry of "Little David," noted healing-evangelist, and Detroit pastor, Mrs. M.D. Beall. Ivan moved among the people, and on the platform among the ministers, in his usual unassuming way, but with a new discernment and intensity of purpose. The spirit of prayer and fasting that had preceded the convention remained to permeate the services.

The prevailing theme of the messages was the concern that "we follow on in progressive revelation, that this move of the Spirit may not end or be hindered as were previous revivals." Conviction and healings characterized the services.

Once when an off-key note was sounded through a visitor's preaching—namely, that the ordinance of communion is unnecessary for those who have the reality of the ritual in their lives—Ivan's handling of the situation was typical. He espoused the necessity of realizing the meaning behind the ordinance, then proceeded with the service. But in the meeting following, he taught on "Reality in Church Ordinances" and included the serving of Communion to the commencement congregation—a beautiful time of together "remembering the Lord's death till He comes."

No doubt some of the accusations leveled at Elim on doctrinal deviations came from just such situations—where, in the interests of unity, an immediate rebuke was withheld, and the matter reserved for later teaching. Such was Ivan's zeal for unity—with *all* the Body of Christ.

Weak leadership? Perhaps, but revival flowed in this absence of over-leading. And who knows but what this might have been a needle's eye to screen out the camels of over-caution that would never have fitted anyway?

Elim lost another staunch friend that spring. Seeley D. Kinne died in California at 92. His strong faith, which all his life had kept him above the limitations of a frail body, saw him through to a triumphant death. Said Ivan, "He had waited with longing expectation for two things—the Latter Rain visitation and the coming of the Lord. He lived to see the beginnings of the first. . . . Through him, the Lord was able to lead me into a deeper life of consecration, and the ministry of the Spirit. . . . He was indeed a 'father in Israel.' "

That early summer, Ivan remained at Elim to hold the reins while Carlton traveled to Cuba with Paul Stutzman, to minister in a convention held in conjunction with the missionaries there. God wonderfully worked in those first few days, and many were saved.

Then one Sunday afternoon, part of the rejoicing congregation, with the converts, piled into cars and a truck, to go to a nearby river for their baptismal service. The missionaries were driving the carloads of people, while one of the national brethren drove the truckload of some fifty lively, praising Christians. Carlton and Paul rode in the back of the truck with them.

As they approached a railroad crossing, they suddenly noticed an oncoming train, then realized the truck could not stop in time. In that awful moment, forty people leaped to their safety, among them Carlton and Paul, but there were nine who were killed, and several injured. Carlton and Paul, with the missionaries, spent the night in ministering to the bereaved families.

"After this, all my burdens will seem as nothing," Carlton wrote home, "when I see with what grace and fortitude the Christians here take this terrible blow. Luisa, one of the women who lost her husband, is preaching the Gospel through tears, to those who come to her house."

The accident was used as a tool by the news media to destroy their Christian testimony, but their opposition became advertisement for the continuing meetings. Miraculous and irrefutable healings took place in increasing number—"God working with them . . . " in the services that followed. The beautiful spirit manifested by the Christians involved in the tragic accident further nullified the malicious work. The whole affair became one of the "all things" which God worked together for glorious good, prospering the work of the Kingdom in Cuba—and sowing seeds of faith for the later T.L. Osborn crusade which made such an impact on the heart of the island.

That camp meeting became another red-letter date in Ivan's life. Through no planning of theirs, the theme of unity through love turned to the missionary cause—God's grand purpose behind this experience of love-flow. And all during that wonderful two weeks of awakened conscience for the needs of the world, God was dealing with Ivan regarding his call to India. Intercessory prayer for nation after nation swept the congregation, and often without invitation, monies were brought to the platform as God laid the needs upon hearts.

Then came the pivotal climax for Ivan. Hands were laid upon him, and he was commissioned by the Spirit to carry the revival message to—India!

With humble gladness, Ivan arose to tell the congregation of his lifetime concern for India, of his despair that it could ever happen, and now the joyous confirmation that indeed it would. As he thus accepted the commission, down in the congregation, Minnie wept and rejoiced for her husband. Though she had no such call as he described, she well knew the confusions that had tried him through the years. He had said to her once, "It must be that God only wants me to train others to go to India, but why—why do I still yearn to go?"

In that glorious final service of the camp, Ivan summed up the portent of the surprise theme of the camp meeting with this challenge: "This visitation of the Holy Spirit must carry a world vision or it will stagnate like other movements. . . . The Golden Text of the Bible has unfolded to me in a new way, 'For God so loved the world that He gave His only begotten Son . . . ' Saints of God, let us awake to the needs of the hour . . . and give ourselves to God for the carrying out of the great burden on His heart in the last of this dispensation."

Also ministering during the camp were Thomas Wyatt, well-known radio minister; Raymond Hoekstra; Alvar Lindskog; William Mulford and Paul Stutzman; Armand Ramseyer; and James and Phyllis Spiers.

Again Ivan and Minnie took to the road, this time traveling with Reverend and Mrs. Daniel Walters, missionaries to India, and ministering in a camp meeting at Baker, Florida. They also held missionary services at Pensacola, and Mobile, Alabama. Ivan's expanded vision of the Body of Christ at work in the world was blessedly contagious, and strengthened the missionary cause.

Two additional developments appeared in that Fall Convention which would seem to point up a basic principle.

The challenge of world vision came across clear and strong, backed by the powerful messages of missionaries present from China, Lebanon, India, and Africa. And notable among the congregation were many who had previously split off over doctrinal differences, but now were drawn back by this mutual hunger for revival. These were part of the blessed unity that prevailed, strengthened no doubt by the mutual focus on world need. Surely the amalgamating force of any enduring unity is the practical recognition of the needs of others.

Students enrollment had reached capacity when Ivan left for the convention of the Pentecostal Fellowship of North America that following week. Such a large number of effervescent youth posed its problems, Ivan well knew, but he was confident that God had provided a capable faculty and all would be well. Newcomers on staff were William Mulford of Indianapolis; Reverend and Mrs. Paul Stewart of Norwich, New York, Lloyd Moulton, formerly of Northwood Bible School in New Hampshire, and two Elim grads.

Ivan headed for Memphis and the PFNA Convention with great anticipation. Not only was he attending because of his membership on the Board of Administration, but also because he was more convinced than ever that God was in the unifying of Pentecostal groups—necessary for the spread of revival. Nor did he feel it in the least inappropriate that he should include in his trip to Memphis a visit to the Latter Rain Pentecostal Church in that city. What Ivan did not know was that already there was antagonism among the delegates and board members against the apparent divisiveness of latter rain and its abuses in many quarters.

Feelings were intensified when the radio blared the news to listening PFNA representatives that "Ivan Spencer, a member of the PFNA Board of Administration, was guest speaker for the Latter Rain Pentecostal Church here in this city!" During the board meeting which followed, questions were raised, and there were reactions. Antagonism toward the "new order Latter Rain revival" was all too evident, especially in those executives who had faced some unChristlike attitudes in men who had been blessed of God in the new visitation. In some instances, congregations were being divided over what came as a blessing from the presence of the Lord—but was now an issue to contend for.

It became more and more apparent to Ivan that there was little sympathy for the visitation, though he shared earnestly with them the blessings the revival had brought to him personally and to the Elim fellowship. Having in mind only the blessedness of his experience of the revival, and failing to realize that these brethren had been exposed to many of the abuses, which he himself deplored and taught against, Ivan finally decided to leave, saying, "It would seem that for the sake of peace, I should resign from the Board. I am very disappointed that this must be so." After embracing each Board member, he walked out, a dejected man.

When he awakened the next morning in his hotel room, there swept over him a deep sense of disappointment over the broken fellowship with brethren he had learned to love. Then suddenly, the Lord began to speak to his heart. It was about the blind man who had been healed, and whose testimony brought him into questioning by the religious leaders. He was reminded of Christ who "suffered without the gate." The next words of Scripture remained with him to become the text for another *Herald* article: "Let us go forth therefore unto Him without the camp, bearing His reproach."

Such hurts do not heal quickly, and Ivan might have felt that being burned once was sufficient. But over the years, Elim's leadership has retained appreciation of the PFNA purposes, and has availed itself of the privilege of again belonging to its stimulating fellowship. Much has been learned since then by all involved, so the matter is a mutual regret, another milestone on Ivan's path of failures and triumphs.

Back at Elim, revival fires burned on. The genuineness of the move of the Spirit among them may be pointed up by one happening shortly after school opened. How it gladdened Ivan to hear about it upon his return!

With many new applications for midyear, and with no room to house them, Carlton had submitted the prayer request that "God would provide the finances needed to expand the facilities to care for these needs." As the students prayed, the spirit of giving gripped them, and spontaneously, they started to give what they could. For a few it was money, but for most it was things, cherished possessions—including watches, rings, musical instruments, and even a motorcycle and a car! The total value was well over four thousand dollars, and the need was met. That midterm, sixteen new students were accepted. It was a happy day for all.

That fall also, Ivan and Carlton joined the thousands from all over the nation who attended the national convention of revival followers at St. Louis, Missouri. It was here that Ivan, Omar Johnson, and Donald Murphy were commissioned to go as a team to India in the month of January. Typically, Ivan's expressed concern was, "We want to minister in the power of the Spirit and in true Christian love and wisdom. Pray for us."

What a thrill to be finally on the way to India, and with Pentecostal brethren of similar persuasion! When their plane landed in Cairo for an eight-hour stopover, Joseph Brown, ever in quest for the Spirit's anointing, came to the airport to be with them. What a blessed time of sharing and prayer it was, and how rewarding to Ivan to witness a renewing from God upon this former student's life. Another visit was made in Lebanon with M.S. Shoucair—then, on to India!

Ivan's reactions to what he encountered there are graphically summed up in these excerpts from his letters from India:

*Madras*— We have already found three national groups among whom we may minister. The poverty is appalling. How the children and the blind flock around us begging . . . have arranged to return here to minister after the convention in south India. . . .

*Kumbanad*— One cannot help but feel sorry for the women of this country; they are in great bondage even in the meetings. In today's services, we are making a way to help them in deliverance from bondages. . . . We just concluded the convention attended by from 8,000-10,000. . . . Now we are holding workers' meetings . . . some 200 pastors from many parts of India. What an opportunity! . . . We three each preach about an hour in each service, and the thermometer is 100-degrees in the shade! But they stand so attentive. What hunger for God! The meetings closed here in a wave of power and glory—your prayers are answered!

*Martandam*— How primitive and what poverty. . . . I slept on a cane cot—I slept because I was too tired to do otherwise! Visited four churches, about 500 believers. God is mightily working among them . . . precious prophecies given over the pastor. . . . The people cannot do enough for me. They give to their poverty—a lime, or an egg, or a piece of money. . . .

Surely revival is on in *Travancore*, and the news is traveling to other parts of India. In *Bangalore* it is cooler, and it was good to get a little rest. A Mohammedan boy and his father, both deaf-mutes, were healed. . . . We are now with P.M. Samuel at *Eluru*. They feed about 2000 at each meal. . . . They sit on the ground in long rows . . . are given a banana leaf and then rice and curry on the leaf . . . eat with their fingers. . . . The people crowd around at every altar call, in such numbers that we cannot pray personally for them all—but still they get saved, healed, and baptized in large numbers. . . . We are so handicapped by not knowing the language. . . .

Here in *Hyderabad*, many deaf and dumb got released through Omar Johnson's ministry. I became much burdened for the many blind. God began to open their eyes, and the crowds have flocked to us night and day. . . . To find oneself in the midst of visitation and have people thronging for salvation, healing, deliverance, the Holy Spirit and the gifts, draws out of one everything that is in him!

*Madras* again. . . . We hired an arbor that would accommodate 6000. . . . Indian Pastors Samuel, Abraham, and Jeevaratnam ministered with us. The place was crowded out . . . hundreds responding every night for salvation, and many receiving the Holy Ghost by the laying on of hands . . . many healings also. I leave soon for Africa, then home, but India is ripe for a mighty visitation. We must have ministered to a thousand Indian apostles, prophets, evangelists, pastors, and teachers. We are impressed both with their educational abilities and their responsiveness to the fresh move of the Holy Spirit.

In Africa, Ivan was met by Bud Sickler at the Nairobi airport and whisked away upcountry to Elim's Bukuria Mission, where Elim missionaries and several hundred Africans were gathered for a convention. What an opportunity for ministry! One after another of the mission-school boys received the Spirit by the laying on of hands. One of the boys was saved, spoke in tongues, then prophesied, all in the same hour! It was not a small comfort to Ivan that nearby stood the schoolhouse erected in memory of his son Paul. These school boys—in a sense, Paul's beneficiaries—were now receiving the spiritual benefits which had been the prime joy of his own simple life.

The services were also a blessing to the missionaries, national pastors, and people, and when Ivan finally left, revival was spreading through the churches.

Meanwhile, Elim had been enjoying continuing visitation. A fresh upsurge came during the January convention, due in part to the ministry of Paul Stutzman of Detroit, now a regular visiting minister at Elim. His foundation-laying teaching ministry had become a great stabilizing influence in many places during these revival days. There was great blessing also from the ministries of Cecil Cousen and Kenneth Mitchell, both of the Apostolic church in Canada, and men of unusual stature in the ministry of the Spirit. The worship in these meetings reached new planes through the Psalm-singing and in praising-through for victories in many areas of need throughout the world.

During this winter also, the school suffered the loss of a faculty member, Blanche Dillenbeck, who had served Elim for nineteen years. She came at first as a nurse, to assist Minnie during an illness and in the delivery of her child, but being spiritually gifted, she remained to teach and assist in the services and with the writing of the *Herald*.

By this time, Elim had become a revival center, a revived oasis, and as such, became responsible for refreshing the drought areas. Several of the Elim personnel were plunged into heavy ministry schedules—wherever the hungry gathered, including in revival churches and at conventions.

Noteworthy, too, was the increasing ministry of Elim graduates among the fellowship churches, with latter rain power attending their ministries. One example of this was Robert Blodget, whose ministering among Elim churches and then in more distant states and Canada was beautifully confirmed with signs following. Today, these confirmations still hold good in his ministry in Mexico, and through the ministries of the national pastors with whom he is associated. Ivan's revival spirit, his willingness to suffer to remain in the stream of revival, was paying rich dividends. The corn of wheat was producing a bountiful harvest.

When school closed that spring with a convention that promised another doubling of enrollment, Ivan and Carlton knew that they faced another Jordan. Should they begin to build all that was needed—a chapel, dormitories, classrooms, and accommodations for married couples—or should they seek another location appropriate to their need? Since Ivan was reluctant to think of indebtedness again, and since he had passed on his leadership mantle to his son, the weight of decision rested on Carlton.

Carlton had never forgotten the nightmare of the Hornell property mortgage. Too, he daily experienced the financial pressures of operational expenses. Yet he knew God was speaking, that there was another mountain for them to take—by faith. There could be no thought of turning back, and they could not remain as they were. They must build, or move where buildings were. Together, the staff prayed—and alone, Carlton wrestled with the problem. It was a heavy load for a young man. As he sought the Lord, he was given a specific Scripture: "Ye have compassed this mountain long enough: turn you northward."

One day, his secretary, June Klotzbach, reminded him, "Remember how my father used to talk about the Genesee Wesleyan Seminary at Lima? He graduated from there in 1912, and after he received the Baptism of the Spirit in 1932—he was still a Methodist preacher—he often would pray that the seminary would be purchased for a Pentecostal Bible school. I think it had been closed for a while at that time. I remember before he died in '47, when our family was on the way down here for camp meeting, daddy stopped there in Lima, got out of the car, marched around that big old administration building seven times, and just praised the Lord for keeping it for a Pentecostal Bible school."

June was laughing now at her reminiscence, and Carlton joined her, both appreciative of the unique expression of faith she had just described. But Carlton was keenly interested.

"Tell me, what was it like?" he asked, and she proceeded to describe the campus and buildings to him. When they turned finally to the business at hand, Carlton was feeling strangely warmed to the idea. He decided to make it a matter of prayer. Come to think of it, it was northward from Hornell—some fifty miles. Was that a coincidence? But was it not still in use as a Methodist school? Doubtful it would be available—and too big a venture, anyway. Nevertheless, he would inquire. Surely the Spirit inspires the prayers of His saints for a purpose—but was this Methodist campus His purpose for Elim?

# 15

*A New Location With New Emphases In Curriculum*

Was it the march of faith, those footfalls echoing through
College Hall corridors, classrooms, chapel and library;
treading the pavement across the shaded hilltop campus to
the large administration building—up, across, down—tra-
versing dormitory halls, rooms, the lounges and offices; then
off across to the barn, the farmhouse, and on to the large
brick building behind the court with the workshop in the
basement, and from its upstairs windows a breathtaking
view—oh, such a view—off across the athletic field to the
city of Rochester, twenty miles away. Then down to the
gymnasium, the footsteps led—was it the march of faith?

A running commentary accompanied this invasion: "What
an awesome building with these huge Ionic pillars—an
architectural gem!" "Whew, look at these classrooms—and
all these blackboards!" "What a beautiful chapel—and this
three-manual organ, does it work?" It does. The Chapel
vibrated with full-orbed tones fingered testingly to the
group's delight. "Isn't this a grand place to study—and all
these bookshelves and books!" "This lounge—how spacious—just right for prayer gatherings, and rainy days

during conventions." "One hundred rooms, you say? But do we need that many?" "Remember, attendance doubled last year!" "How spread out and light this dining room is—the kitchen, too—ours in the basement at Hornell are so dark!"

Then a squeal of delight as the gymnasium doors were thrown open—"Won't the students love this?—I mean, well, if God wants us to have it—"

Carlton Spencer smiled, and agreed. Objectivity wasn't going to be easy with all these glowing remarks from his camp meeting friends and fellow staff members. Perhaps it was a mistake to spy out the land when he still was not completely sure, hadn't even talked purchase price yet. These remarks were actually frightening, and suddenly he felt they must have prayer and commit it all into the Lord's hands. "C'mon," he called to the group, "let's move on outside for prayer before we leave."

To the scant summer crew residing on the college campus, the sight of that little huddle on the lawn—praying and praising God in true Pentecostal fashion—must have been astounding, or perhaps amusing. It wouldn't have been, however, to the earliest inhabitants of the seminary, revival followers of Finney's day who were training to spread revival fires throughout the nation. Unknown to the college-crew onlookers, the fires burning in the hearts of these strangers well equipped them for belonging on this revival-born campus.

Back at camp meeting in Hornell, the report was a glowing one. God further confirmed His leading to Lima, and the congregation gave generously—$8,000. Stanley Frodsham's challenge in regard to God's purpose for Elim and this new campus was both thought-provoking and exciting. He recounted the story of Reformation persecutions and especially the refugees for whom Count Zinzendorf had opened his estate at Herrnhut. They had come from different countries and environments and had little knowledge of the

Word, or the crucified life. There was soon dissension among them.

God gave the Count a word of wisdom. "Take the words of Jesus and seek by His grace to obey them—especially the new commandment, to love one another as Christ loved you." Then he challenged them with the vision God had given him, "To win for the Lamb that was slain the reward of His sufferings." Thus began the Moravian Movement.

Said Frodsham, "There was a glorious outpouring of the Spirit as these refugees agreed to seek to live by the words of Christ, and a prayer meeting began that continued for over a hundred years. Missionaries went forth, some even selling themselves as slaves so they could better reach the slaves for Christ. . . . When John Wesley visited Herrnhut, after being born again in a Moravian prayer meeting in England, he noticed the great care they had for all their new converts; spiritual fathers and mothers were designated to take watchful care of every newborn 'lamb.' In later days when he had large numbers of converts, he sought that they should have the same watchful care that he had seen given to the converts at Herrnhut."

Frodsham compared early Methodism, and that of Finney's day, with that represented by the Genesee Junior College. Then he added, "but God is graciously sending latter rain revival. . . . The vision is to prepare workers for the gathering of the Harvest in this eleventh hour. . . . The Elim student body doubled last year. . . . Let us pray that the Lord will provide the funds for this campus, and that *Lima may become another Herrnhut where God's Spirit is constantly outpoured, where prayer shall ascend to God day and night, and from which hundreds of missionaries may go forth to win for the Lamb that was slain the reward of His sufferings.*"

Before such a high standard as this, Elim stands dwarfed, humbled—still unfulfilled. But praise God for His grace in continually visiting Elim with the spirit of prayer and intercession, with revival and revelation; and in pouring through faculty and staff, though imperfectly, the love of Jesus for both the individual student of its family and the lost multitudes of the world. Like the apostle Paul, Elim has not yet attained, but may it ever strive to "apprehend that for which it has been apprehended."

For Ivan, the proposed purchase of the campus was a deepening concern. One evening he worried aloud about it to Minnie. "Minnie, Carlton's taking an awful load on himself."

"Not on himself, Ivan, he has the whole school and fellowship behind him—and the many confirmations to encourage him. But he does need our prayers."

"You know, Minnie, as I walked that campus with Carlton last week, I, too, felt really excited, but now that I'm home, and facing that $175,000 figure—I'm not so sure. Why that's nearly five times the cost of this property!" Ivan was pacing the floor now, anxiety written on his face. Minnie watched him apprehensively. He continued, "The operating costs alone for all those buildings are unthinkable. Of course, there is the ninety-acre farm to help with food demands—but it's a load on the boy, Minnie, a terrible load."

Minnie stood and looked him squarely in the eye. "A load on *him*, you say? Just remember that, Ivan; it's not *your* responsibility. Your mantle is now on Carlton, and with our prayer-backing, and the cooperation of the members of the Body who stand with us, God will see him—us—through. But physically, you can't take going under that load again." Now it was Minnie's turn to look worried.

Ivan chuckled, gave her a peck on the cheek, then went back to his books. But he sighed as he absentmindedly flipped the pages. It wasn't easy to slip out of the picture—even when the going was rough.

The crisis came when the Genesee Junior College board convened in Rochester to deliberate the sale of the campus. Carlton was present for the interview; accompanying him was his close friend Lloyd Moulton, an Elim teacher and maintenance supervisor. Inexperienced in such weighty business matters, they approached, with some dismay, the hotel where the board met. To believe God in a camp meeting crowd, where faith ran high and offerings flowed freely in a spirit of hilarious giving, was one thing; to be as confident before a committee of hard-headed businessmen, lawyers, a Methodist bishop and his superintendents, was another.

Among the many questions leveled at the fearful young principal of Elim were, "What do you Pentecostals believe, anyway?" and "What are your views of Oral Roberts?" (Certainly no one at that meeting dreamed future years would find that famous evangelist joining the Methodist denomination.) As for the answers, Carlton made no great showing—frightened and nervous, his voice had sunk to a whisper.

The interview finally over, Carlton joined Lloyd down in the lobby as the decision was being reached in the room above them. There had been months of prayer, heart-searching, and deliberation; then weeks of careful, prayerful correspondence. Now the hour had come, and there were only chilling fears and doubts.

"Lloyd, I'm not so sure now that we ought to make this move. Hope they decide against us—how about you?"

"Well, we prayed about it and I really thought it was the thing to do; but when I think of that $175,000. . . . "

A door opened behind them. Carlton sprang up uncertainly. After all, with such a comparatively low bid, the verdict could easily be negative. It was Augustus Mertz, the elderly chairman of the Methodist board. He smiled and placed a friendly hand on Carlton's shoulder, "It's all yours, son."

Carlton crumpled weakly back into the chair—this was too much. He managed a smile as he replied, "I was afraid you'd say that." The keen old man detected the quailing of faith in the trauma of the moment. "Where is your faith, young man?" The tender rebuke steadied Carlton and he drank in the words of encouragement. When they parted, Carlton was ready to sustain the staggering new load— buoyed by the wise counsel of an old layman who claimed little knowledge of the supernatural realm of the Spirit, but who used that little to full advantage.

Only later did Carlton discover the intricacy of the Spirit's design in that epochal meeting. Long before he stood in front of that board, Carlton had befriended an old man in an hour of need. Only God knew that one of the lawyers sitting on that board was that same old man's son-in-law, George Cooke—who in subsequent years has served as Elim's attorney and advisor, at virtually no charge.

With his father's mantle drawn closely about him, Carlton penned these words for the *Herald* readers—Elim's friends and prayer-partners:

In every time of visitation, new and greater challenges are pressed upon those who purpose to move on in God in His forward leadings. . . . God has likewise dealt with us, revealing the place He wants us to fill in the preparation of young people for this harvest hour. . . . At the beginning of this year God gave me, "Ye have dwelt long enough on this mount . . . turn you northward." . . . Near the end of the school year it became evident that there must be a venture in expansion far beyond anything we had previously considered. . . . News reached us that the Methodists were contemplating selling their campus in Lima, just forty-five minutes north of us! . . . God began to confirm that this was His leading . . . through many individuals . . . scriptures . . . prophecies. God gave us the figure of $175,000 as the price we were to offer. . . . Preparation is now being made for transfer of the title. . . . A tremendous undertaking . . . rest only comes in following Him as He has so definitely led. *A deeper conviction has gripped our hearts that this venture is part of God's great plan* for the preparation of young people with the message of the Gospel of the Kingdom . . . for endtime harvest.

To chronicle those trying days of waiting for legal procedures, when again and again it seemed the sale would not go through, then those hectic days of moving and setting up immediately for the fall convention of 1951, would fill a volume. As wonderful as were the answers to prayer involved, the supplying of finances, and the teamwork of the Elim family, we must subordinate the telling to the bigger story of the onward goings of God in revival.

Meanwhile Ivan and Minnie set off for the mideastern states, to minister among churches and conventions. Though blessings abounded, Ivan detected threads of error being woven into the glorious fabric of God's visitation, and his heart was stirred to resistance. Arriving home in September, he went to work to reinforce his spoken admonitions with his editorial, "Take Heed unto the Doctrine." Note the timeliness of his words:

Because we are in a fresh visitation of the Holy Spirit we by no means have license to ignore the old landmarks of our faith, nor consider them as traditional and of no value to this fresh move of the Spirit. . . . Every revival makes Jesus more real, the shedding of His blood more precious, and the victories of the Cross more outstanding. . . . There is an urgent need to sound a warning to those in this fresh visitation. Many of the errors of other visitations during this Church age are rising again . . . presented as part of the revival, as though it could not continue without them. . . .

Let us mention some of the great doctrines of the

Bible now under attack: . . . It is true that there is a return of Jesus and a manifestation of Him in and through His Body, but this does not give us license to cast to the wind the precious teaching of His personal, visible return to the earth—"this same Jesus . . . shall so come in like manner as ye have seen Him go into heaven." . . . Another erroneous doctrine . . . that all the prophecies regarding the restoration of Israel as a nation apply to spiritual Israel—the Church. The Jew is still God's timepiece. . . .

The "restoration" (of apostolic power and glory) does not give us license to parade the false doctrine of former years; that is, that everything is to be restored, even the devil, the fallen angels and the wicked dead. . . . We read in Acts 3 that the heavens must receive Jesus "until the times of restitution (restoration) of all things *which God hath spoken by the mouth of His holy prophets . . .* " and *only* all of that which the prophets have spoken! Heaven is eternal and hell which was prepared for the devil and his angels is also eternal. . . .

There is much teaching today regarding a select company out of the Church—"Bride," "Man-child," "Sons of God. ". . . The whole Church has never measured up to this standard . . . but most will agree that God will have a people who will measure up. . . . However there are so many variations of teaching that the tendency is to mystify and distort truth, thus bringing division in the Body. *Can we not hold in the background such teachings that divide the Body of Christ?*

Significantly, a week of prayer preceded the fall convention and school opening in Lima. Sacrificing precious hours from moving and settling to make room for Elim's priority—seeking God for His blessing—proved to be that necessary heart preparation for a glorious beginning on the new campus. When the convention began in October, people arrived from every direction, outnumbering any such previous gatherings. College Hall Chapel, seating 450, could never contain the rejoicing throngs that overflowed the campus.

Volunteers worked feverishly to repair the long-closed Methodist Church in town to accommodate the weekend attendance. The dedication service on Sunday saw the building packed to the doors and overflowing onto the lawn. How the Spirit witnessed in that service, confirming that the hand of the Lord was in the school's new venture!

Again the theme of world harvest prevailed. Among those reporting from distant lands was P.M. Samuel of India, his dark-skinned patriarchal appearance and flowing white robes adding impressively to the scene. Others included John Owen of Europe, Milford Kirkpatrick of the Orient, Fred Poole recently of England, W. Gummer of French Canada, and Ivan Spencer—expansive and glowing in the excitement of God's fresh move for Elim, and in his growing conviction that his vision for worldwide revival was fast becoming a reality.

School opened with eighty students, and prospects of more at midterm. A new brochure was printed and circulated regarding the school in its new location, and reaffirming its objectives:

## Spiritual Objectives

The leaders and staff of Elim . . . are seeking to meet the challenge of revival by sending forth "able ministers of the New Testament." In view of the fact that it is possible to train students until they are "letter-perfect" and yet void of true spiritual understanding—and that intellectual attainment can never take the place of the Spirit of God—we are seeking to place the chief emphasis on the spiritual growth of the individual. We covet the spirit of revelation in the classroom, more than human scholarship. We aim to give each student opportunity for the exercising of the gifts of the Spirit in the Body of Christ.

One innovation that first year at Lima was a midwinter, four-week short term course, for Christian workers seeking further teaching and encouragement in revival ministry. Guest teachers joined the resident faculty in classroom ministry. Afternoons were spent with the Christian workers in prayer and ministry by the Spirit to personal needs; evening services were attended by all, a real source of spiritual refreshing. This same thrust remains today in the form of a week of prayer in January and a one-week ministers' seminar.

Though he was hampered physically in times of stress by a nervous heart ailment and by a lifelong sinus condition that was a continual irritation in his preaching ministry, Ivan's courage was still high for usefulness in world harvest. This intrepid pioneer for revival must yet see more distant shores before he could surrender the torch to younger hands. Opportunity came that fall when he accompanied his daughter Ruth and her husband, George Veach, and Elim grad, Celia Brand, now in Peru, to the island of Cuba.

Sixto and Ruth (Garate) Lopez met them on their arrival in Havana. Seeing Sixto Lopez brought back to Ivan's mind vivid memories of the boy's coming to Elim nearly twenty years before, a stowaway Puerto Rican from a broken home. Ivan had met him in a basement Pentecostal church in Brooklyn. He knew the boy took in little of his sermon but seemed keenly interested when he spoke of the purposes of God and Joel's promise that God would pour out His Spirit upon all flesh. Seeking him out after the service, Ivan had asked, "When are you coming to Bible school?" That settled it for Sixto, a new convert, knowing little of the Bible or even of the English language. Ivan accepted him into Elim, little realizing the revival firebrand he had in the making.

Sixto's glowing countenance and animated discussion of his work as they traveled back into Matanzas province in his little jeep, now thrilled Ivan. Could he have seen ahead twenty years, he would have been even more amazed, for Sixto's radio ministry already begun in Cuba was to spread over a number of the countries of Latin America, winning thousands to the Lord and being the instrument of healing for multitudes.

Arriving in the city of Matanzas, Ivan and his party were welcomed by Peter and Marion Seda. Marion was Leslie Spencer's oldest daughter. It was a grand time of reunion and sharing of the joys and sorrows of their ministries.

The next two weeks were spent in touring the back country of Matanzas province, ministering in the newly established churches of the primitive villages and in Sixto's city church. They also met some of the faithful, fiery Cuban workers who held the future of Cuba's revival in their hands. Then, ignoring physical weakness, Ivan accompanied George and Ruth, and Celia and the Lopezes, to the seaport town of Cardenas, for an evangelistic campaign. How Ivan's heart ached for the many villages en route—poverty and religiosity a dual curse upon the daily lives of the villagers. Cardenas was a beautiful resort city of comparative affluence, but equally heartbreaking in its obvious sinfulness.

In the nights that followed, Ivan was thrilled to see the people stream toward the outdoor platform in response to the full gospel altar call, and God healed, saved, and filled these sin-cursed lives with holy joy. Daytimes were spent in ministry among the homes, and again the power of God brought deliverances.

Ivan was greatly stirred one day when an old man whom he'd just led to the Lord told him, "Forty years ago my wife was saved through Pentecostal missionaries, who left soon after. . . . Neither I nor anyone else would listen to her, so she prayed all these years for Pentecostal missionaries to return and get us converted. . . . She died last year, still not seeing her desire—and I not caring until now."

That evening Ivan wrote a stirring article for the next *Herald*. It concluded,

God heard the heartcry of that Christian and sent us to Cardenas—no wonder He is so mightily working here! But why could not God have answered that prayer sooner? Dear Reader, you help me answer this question, 'Why did not someone hear that cry during those forty years, even you or I? . . .'

As the Cardenas campaign drew to a close, the Veaches remained to establish a church there. Ivan left with exciting thoughts of being part of Cuba's harvest hour.

Limonar, just thirty miles inland from Cardenas, was a small backward town, and a center for spiritist activities. Early in Sixto's ministry, a spiritist medium of that town was converted, healed, and Spirit-filled. One by one, the patron saints stacked on shelves in a corner of her home disappeared—Sixto noting and rejoicing. Her Chinese husband did not complain until one day, the ugliest, most evil idol of all—his potbellied Buddha—was gone. Luisa produced the Buddha from under the bed, trembling before her husband's wrath, but pleading, "Can't you see what the Christian's God has done for me? Why do we need this Buddha anymore?" Reluctantly, he gave in. He couldn't refuse the evidence of the superiority of his wife's God. On Sixto's next visit, there was an idol bonfire in the former medium's backyard, and now Luisa was a flaming witness to her own people. She not only held meetings in her own home in Limonar, but also in neighboring villages, assisted by Elim's missionaries, Thelma and Esther Wilhelm, and Ina Garate—Elizabeth's mother and a veteran missionary with world conquest in her heart.

It was to this town that Ivan traveled with Sixto one day. He was challenged to note what God had done, and what must yet be done to rout the powers of darkness entrenched here. His heart was stirred as the ladies shared with him the horrors of the cultist activities, even to child sacrifice. Surely the power of God held the only answer for such demonic powers as these. He was again stimulated to believe for even greater Elim involvement in Cuba.

Then as time drew near to return to the States, Ivan's good friend, Paul Stutzman, and a team of anointed revival ministers arrived in Cuba for tent crusades at the leading of the Lord. With them came word that others from New York City and the midwest were soon to arrive for ministry, also at the Lord's leading.

Truly, God's time had come for Cuba. Ivan left the island rejoicing, and bringing with him back to Elim a token of God's continuing purpose—a young Cuban worker seeking training for a revival ministry in his own land.

That spring the commencement convention witnessed thirteen graduates receiving their diplomas. Among them were Ivan's daughter, Faith (soon to marry Clifton Cartland and with him to later serve on Elim's staff and as a pastor's wife); and Leslie's daughter, Edith (soon also to serve on staff and later to serve in pastorates with her husband, Noah Stoltzfus—an Elim grad of '58).

That summer, Elim hosted a Camp Farthest Out, with an old friend, J. Rufus Moseley, as one of its ministering leaders. Since one of the C.F.O.'s distinctives is recreational prayer, each morning the villagers and Elim's traditional-type Pentecostal friends were treated to daily demonstrations of devotion. The spreading campus lawns became an elevated and noticeable amphitheater for their devout calisthenic activities. Needless to say, Elim's willingness to host this not-too-well-understood assortment of evangelical, liturgical, liberalist, and in some cases, cultist, following of the hungry-hearted, brought criticisms from several quarters.

In the course of the camp, Rufus Moseley's quiet but earnest reporting of God's work in his own life found a responding spark of hunger in some attending his classes. They clamored for instructions on how to receive what he had, but Moseley wisely answered, "I am only a reporter." Finally, the C.F.O. leaders consented to a closed session on the Baptism in the Spirit, under the leadership of Carlton Spencer.

The hours behind those closed doors to Elim's library in College Hall became another fulfillment of God's promise, "And I will pour out my Spirit upon all flesh." What a glorious time of rejoicing it was! Again Elim was only following its inherent tendency to fellowship the hungry, regardless of cost to reputation—and for some, Elim had no reputation to lose!

Perhaps the years have proven the rightness of such an attitude, for Elim has continued to be a revival oasis for many isolated hungry groups over the years, and always an influence for Christ and His Word to the untaught among them.

When school opened that fall, a high school department had been added, and the Bible school curriculum took on a distinct Christian education emphasis which was sparked by a growing need among the churches. Sunday school workshops and clinics were held throughout the area, staffed by Elim personnel and including students, for their training. Specialists in the field were called in to assist, though a dominant revival correlation was obvious.

This inevitably led to a home missions emphasis, long overdue. It was a welcome balance to the farsighted World

Harvest thrust and, in the long-range view, an essential to it.

These innovations, however, inspired a fear in Ivan, who was now somewhat unrelated to daily school activities. Nor was he as aware of needs among Elim's churches as he might have been were he not so preoccupied with travel among latter rain conventions, as well as overseas. On each return home, any changes in procedure were immediately suspect, Ivan not knowing the evolving needs which prompted them. With reservations, he would acquiesce to explanations made at board meetings. No doubt his caution was a needed factor in these days of growing pains for Elim.

The following year, with the emphases of home missions and Christian education continuing, Elim added two more strong men to its faculty, both missionaries with worldwide revival vision—Edward Miller of Argentina and Elmer Frink of Nigeria, who was also one of the early leaders in the Detroit latter rain revival. This meant a heightened missions emphasis, with curriculum additions necessary to the strengthening of both departments.

What a joy to Ivan and Minnie when in the spring of 1953 they saw their daughter Eva (Spencer) Butler off for Africa. Her persistent faithfulness in home missions and constant affirmation of God's calling to missionary work in Africa made a way for her and her two children to become part of Elim's Bukuria Mission personnel. Her later work with the fierce Masai tribe, long closed to missionaries and officials alike, has carved her name upon Africa's list of missionary pioneers. The young Morani tribesmen (warriors), now Bible school trained and pastoring Masai churches, are living proof of her calling.

Accompanying Eva to the field was Edith Knoll, an Old Elim missionary to Liberia who had buried her husband on the mission field twenty-five years before, and was now returning for her second term to Kenya. She literally poured out her lonely life for Kenyan schoolboys at Bukuria, refusing furloughs and, in 1969, dying in the land of her adoption. One of her boys is today an Elim student, in training for ministry among his own Kuria tribespeople.

With a more full-orbed spiritual perspective—and strong, matching personnel—Elim should have leaped forward to its goals in God. But the enemy has a way of triggering the wheels of progress, necessitating miracles of intervention and meanwhile, refining and strengthening those goals.

One reversal in plans was the lessening, rather than increasing, of student enrollment, due to difficulties that were developing within the revival movement through doctrinal errors and schisms. Elim's open rejection of such errors as already described—plus an unwholesome over-emphasis on grace that twisted and weakened the truth of sanctification—caused the loss of support from certain churches, both in their young people and in finances. Again, Ivan's uncompromising stand for truth, Carlton standing with him, stood the test. Elim continued on in the old paths that had been both biblically and experientially proven.

The saying, "God's man, doing God's will, in God's way, will never lack God's support" may apply to a school as well. Elim proved this in ways that could fill volumes, over the years of recurring trial and loneliness, of everpresent mortgage payments and continual last-minute meeting of need. Again and again, in impossible situations, God came through with financial provision, the $3,000 monthly budget account book becoming a chronicle of miracles—nay, rather, of God's faithfulness.

On December 30, 1953, Ivan left for another trip to India, ministering in Africa and Europe en route. Accompanying him was his close friend Paul Stutzman, and John Sitko, another revival minister. A missionary candidate for Kenya, George Lindsay—an Elim grad of that year—also traveled with them as far as Africa. Ivan's trip diary gives telling glimpses of his experiences:

On way to New York City stopped in at Vern's . . . continuing in prayer and fellowship with Jesus—very determined to apply myself to God and my God-given ministries. . . . Parting with my loved one was a bit hard. . . . On plane had good times in prayer. . . . God gave me Heb. 11. for New Year—a year for the exercise of mighty faith. . . . Arrived London . . . Cecil Cousen spent the day with us in fellowship and sight-seeing. . . . James Salter came at night—he is a hungry soul. . . . On to Africa . . .

Bud Sickler not at Nairobi to meet us but sent tickets for Mombasa . . . long, hard ride . . . saw much wild-life . . . arrived next day at their nice apartment . . . heat excessive . . . rested . . . had splendid meeting at night, many coming for salvation. . . . Africans, Indians, Arabs and Whites attending. . . . preached Baptism and Healing . . . on a trip through reserve saw buffalo, elephant, hippo and many kinds of antelope . . . took a trip on reef today . . . meetings continue to grow in power—about 15 received Holy Spirit one night . . . en route to Bukuria, ran through cloud of locusts. . . . met by Art and May Dodzweit, Sister Knoll and Eva . . . good to see the kiddies. . . .

*Bukuria* . . . Sunday God healed many in bush country . . . in Arombi church many saved, healed, filled with Spirit—over 200 present. . . . tent meetings going rather slow . . . some disappointment . . . better on Sunday . . . held Bible teaching periods with African pastors . . . saw barriers of misunderstanding melt, true sign of revival . . . ordained Opunga and laid hands on many . . . hard to part with Eva . . . visited Lichty's en route to Nairobi . . . held meetings and again many saved, healed and filled with Spirit.

. . . Talked with Carlton on "ham" station at Eldoret . . . on to Nairobi . . . off for India. . . .

India again—land of cows, crows and crowds . . . none to meet us . . . traveled by plane, then train, to Bezwada . . . hard time to find Brother Samuel . . . good meetings on Sunday and Monday, then on to Eluru . . . very hot . . . meetings singularly marked by deep heart-hunger . . . thousands gather . . . many here have leprosy and elephantiasis, are blind, deaf and dumb, lame . . . many healed, saved, filled. . . . some prayed till 2:00 A.M. for the sick. . . . little boy pressed on me to lay hands on him and pray . . . did so . . . noticed as I prayed some disturbance under my hands but kept praying . . . when finished I found I had prayed for not one but many such boys passing under my hands . . . very touched by their hunger . . this morning preached on Samson. . . . Brother Samuel, founder of this work in Telugu field, much moved upon. . . . God is dealing with us all. . . . On last day arose at 4:30 A.M. to lay on hands for receiving the Holy Spirit. Many, many received . . . 121 baptized in water . . . their business meetings hindered but God overruled. . . .

At Gudivada some saved and healed . . . at A.S. Paul's place over a thousand had gathered . . . wonderful meetings . . . on to Warengal . . . very hot . . . no freedom in night services—tested. . . . pleasant stay at Hyderabad—cooler . . . exceptional meetings . . . marvelous answers to prayer . . . many turned to God. . . . at Madras crowds not like three years ago . . . opposition by both Hindus and communists growing toward preaching of gospel . . . three services a day . . . extremely hot . . . can appreciate hardships of missionaries under this kind of intensive effort . . . one needs to know he is sent of God to persevere . . . heat, bugs, inconveniences, problems always connected with Christian work in foreign country—all call for not only one's best, but the grace of God. . . . at Trivandrum meetings going well but not well attended. . . .

At Bangalore Carl Butler met us . . . held meeting with Assembly of God then on to Mysore and Brother Barnabas . . . here three local papers oppose us. . . . it is India's day of visitation but the doors are closing to foreigners . . . evidence that our movements are being watched . . . pray the Lord will protect. . . . Delhi—difficult services . . . attended Stanley Jones meeting at night, very good . . . services some better now with a breaking among denominationals . . . leave tomorrow for Lebanon. . . .

Arrived Beirut . . . rough trip from Karachi . . . found Shoucair . . . held meetings with them nights. . . . 50 came to the Lord tonight . . . having meetings in refugee camps . . . a profitable week. . . .

Switzerland, Chateau d' Oex, and Hotel Rosat (John Owen's "revival" center and school) . . . what a beautiful country. . . . resting and ministering to students . . . they have spirituality. . . . in Germany, good meetings . . . much hunger here . . . pastor was converted in Russia . . . entertained by elderly sister who lost husband and son in war . . . precious time in Zurich with group of 400 praying for revival. . . . in Germany visited a man in deception of demon power, getting demons converted! This land has much devil work. Some have meetings in cemeteries to convert the dead! In Stuttgart good meetings . . . city much in ruins from war . . . back at Chateau d' Oex . . . held classes with students on Romans and I Corinthians . . . the parting was sweet. . . .

On to London . . . spent time in parks today. . . . in Bradford spoke on Feast of Tabernacles and Intercession . . . leave for London, and home, tomorrow. . . .

Ivan arrived home spiritually quickened but physically depleted, and as in the aftermath of his first trip, required months of rest before being able to devote himself to his home labors.

# 16

*Willow Flexibility For A Complex Growth*

No one who attended that camp meeting of 1954 could ever forget it. World Prayer Conquest was its theme, and the actual outworking of that theme was amazing.

It was a deep and sweeping move of the Spirit, which had its beginnings in January when the week of prayer lengthened into four weeks. Classes were suspended while the Spirit taught rich lessons day after day in the realm of intercession. What heart searchings and humblings, empowerings and revelations; a going ever deeper in order to climb ever higher in this realm of effectual prayer. Many were the choruses born during these weeks of prayer with the students. Probing hours were spent together in reading aloud whole chapters of Scripture.

Then the ministerial prayer fellowship that preceded the spring convention in May adjourned with plans for another such meeting the following month. Said Carlton, "We cannot continue on the momentum of the past. We must ever meet God afresh."

As planned, the ministers and Christian workers met again at Elim in late June, preceding the camp meeting. This time the missionaries overseas had been alerted to be in prayer. Again the spirit of grace and supplications was poured out upon them. The crowds that gathered the following week for camp meeting simply fed the flames of the Spirit's intercessory bonfire.

The usual early morning prayer hour often extended through the morning Bible study. Breakfast and lunch were easily forgotten by those caught up in prayer. Ministries during afternoon and evening services included reports of missionaries and Invasion Team members, presenting the urgent needs and triumphs of their respective fields. Ivan also shared the fresh burdens on his heart from his recent travels to Africa, India, and Europe. These worldwide challenges sparked more intercessions, often agonizing soul travail, wrestling with the powers of darkness in various nations. In such intercessions, Russia, China, and other closed countries were entered by faith. Often travail would erupt into glorious waves of praise as victory was assured.

When Ivan arose one such afternoon to address the congregation he had fathered into existence just thirty years before, he was given their undivided attention. Trembling from weakness and emotion, he began to tell of that first camp meeting in Endwell in 1924—of the flame of revival that was Elim's beginning—and of the fresh outpouring that had begun five years ago for most of them.

He paused a moment, then continued with increasing fervency, "This revival flame depends upon the praying, prevailing Christian. Is it to die out, leaving behind the consciousness that it could have been revival, or is it to spread until it reaches the 'all flesh' of Joel's mighty prophecy? The Holy Ghost bids us today to fan these flames with Holy Ghost prayers, intercessions . . . with carefulness yet zeal. . . . God would raise up many who are devoted to revival, to fanning the flame, until all men everywhere have been touched by the purifying, energizing flame of the Holy Ghost."

In the moments that followed, there were many rededications to "fan the flame." God also led in ministry to personal needs, by the Spirit, many being ministered unto that they in turn might minister. In such an atmosphere, it was inevitable that testimonies would come forth at every opportunity, revealing transformed lives, miracles of healing, and a move of the Spirit among the youth of the camp.

Nor was the home area neglected, for state after state became the focus of prayer as representatives present expressed their burden for their own communities. There was also a challenge to prayer-prepared witness throughout these communities when camp meeting would conclude.

"Lord, send rain in this time of the latter rain" was the prayer common to all. Prayer battles grew in momentum, and after one evening service, over 150 remained in prayer throughout the night. "They who do business in great waters; these see the works of God, and His wonders in the deep." How rich the dividends from such an investment—to those souls who will press in and dwell deep in the purposes of God. And what release from the strictures of self-interest; what healing from petty indifferences; what strength of unity is thus developed.

Before camp meeting closed, these prayer-warriors were hearing of God's moving in parts of the world for which they had been led by the Spirit to pray. And such sacrificial praying produced sacrificial giving, the greatest Elim had known up to this time.

That fall Elim added strong prayer-backing to their staff through the ministries of the Stanley Frodshams and the A.O. Moores, who took up residence on campus. The Edward Millers had returned to South America, to reap an increasing harvest through the spreading Argentine revival.

A prayerful analysis of the needs of the Elim churches and pastors resulted in the release of Cliff Cartland to travel among the churches as youth worker; the providing of matured ministry to visit throughout the fellowship, giving the encouragement and help needed to pastors and congregations; and the setting up of a prayer vigil at the school whereby pastors might receive prayer-backing for specific needs—this ministry coming under the direction of the Stanley Frodshams. Now surely it would seem that Elim was invincibly equipped for harvest conquest.

As one of the matured ministries provided to assist the churches, Ivan went back to his circuit-riding labors, delighting most of all in the struggling pioneer works pastored by young Elim graduates. One such church was in Lockwood, New York, a small village in a mountainous area. The pastor was a senior at Elim, commuting to finish his schooling.

As Ivan drove into the churchyard, he recognized the building to be an old one-room schoolhouse, a vivid reminder of his own pioneer days. He was warmly received by the young man and led up into the schoolhouse attic, now remodeled into a livable apartment.

"Tell me, son, what brought you here?" Ivan was feeling for that expression of vision he longed to hear.

"Well, when school closed last spring, I felt God had work for me to do, and that I shouldn't go home to a job for the summer. I stayed on at school waiting for the opening, and it came. It seems that a Christian lady visiting her daughter here, saw the need for a Sunday school and got permission to use this schoolhouse. She had been conducting it herself for a year when she called Elim asking to be relieved. It was really ready to become a church when I came. Another senior has been helping me, and several have been saved; some have been filled with the Spirit. There have been several miraculous healings, too."

"From the way it sounds, you must be getting crowded in that little room down there," Ivan observed, enjoying his visit immensely.

"Oh, we are; and already we are negotiating for a house that will readily convert into a larger chapel, with Sunday school rooms." Taking Ivan into his cubicle of an office, the young man showed him a large map of Tioga county tacked on the wall over his desk. Strings led out from the town of Tioga to each of the eight county districts.

"We plan to open a church in each of these districts, using closed schoolhouses for meeting places. We are opening soon in Mt. Pleasant here. It, too, is an old closed schoolhouse but can easily be made into a neat little chapel."

"Just a minute, son—who do you mean by 'we'? You two students?"

"The church and us together. Everyone is pitching in. You should just see their enthusiasm!"

Ivan laughed and clapped him on the shoulder. "Enthusiasm's contagious, young man. Just see that you keep it under the anointing, that's all. You really love what you're doing, don't you?"

"Sure do," he answered, jumping up to pace the floor. "And you know what gave me a real thrill last week? I've already got a student for Elim! This young fellow got saved a few months ago—he's a great guy, really, you'll like him. Well, he's sure now that he is to be a preacher, and that means Bible school. He's all set for coming next term."

When Ivan headed for home a few hours later, he drove in the glow of successful parenthood. He had just witnessed a clear case of spiritual reproduction, discipleship in its highest form. Such knowledge was sweet to his taste . . . just wait till Minnie heard about this!

Ivan's refreshing vision of missions at home somewhat relieved his fears that its overemphasis would detract from the world harvest vision. But there were other trends that

198

concerned him, such as the increase of academic demands upon the students, a noticeable contrast to his previous very simple curriculum, easily dropped for weeks at a time in deference to other duties, or prayer.

"Do you really think, Carlton, that training for revival ministry necessitates all these new subjects? So much educational training can make a student forget all about revival. I tell you, we're getting too academic." Ivan's voice rose tremblingly.

"But dad, there's not a thing unspiritual about any subject we teach. You know how much help the churches need along a lot of lines, and many of our graduates didn't get the subjects that could have helped them now. The students can stand to study a little harder, and the Lord is moving in our midst—in the classes, too."

"Perhaps. But Carlton, I'm afraid you are missing the best."

"I—I know you are afraid, dad. I really appreciate your interest and prayers, and I will watch out for things, really." Thus ended another session on Ivan's fears of the trends. There would be similar conversations on other worrisome matters, such as an increasing association with non-Pentecostal organizations, and the opening of Methodist pastorates to Elim graduates.

Ivan's lifelong openness to ministry from any source helped him to hold no antagonism toward this encroaching denominational influence, but again he feared for the students. Of course, he realized there were the advantages of an enriched fellowship, and expanded horizons for service, but an overwhelming of non-Pentecostal influence could be dangerous. An Elim graduate out on his own, pliable to any influence in his youth and inexperience, could be swallowed up!

"But Joel's prophecy promises that the Spirit will be poured out upon *all flesh*. That means people like these must be reached somehow with the revival message. Isn't this one way to reach them—supply these liberal church pulpits with our young men who have a genuine experience?" Ivan was thus reminded in a board meeting discussion, and he had to admit to the logic—but still he feared.

Actually, experience later taught that there was truth on both sides. Perhaps it also taught that pushing any set method, to the disregard of the need of individual personal guidance, is moving out of step with God.

Then there was the trend toward further education—the encouraging of college attendance for students whose calling to pulpit ministry made advisable studies not offered in Elim's curriculum. Ivan feared that college attendance might cause the students to lose sight of the priority of anointing, a loss which could be fatal to a revival ministry. Thus again he saw his basic calling—to train youth for endtime revival ministry—threatened.

Having been the leader and decision-maker for Elim for so many years, Ivan was particularly vulnerable to such fears, and his lifelong passion for revival made him especially sensitive to each administrative move. The pain of his early experience in the seminary was yet a vivid memory, and his acquaintance with other schools that had lost sight of their original objectives gave him reason for concern.

Certainly his insistent voice during Elim's transition period in leadership served to keep the vision of endtime revival before their eyes. Redefinement of purpose, and extension of objectives, were essential, however, for adapting to a changing world. The implementing of revival ministry must be as flexible as the times.

Another cause for concern was the increasing of faculty—so many new faces, all loving him and loved by him, but do they have Elim's vision? he wondered. It was difficult to conceive that they would.

Ivan would confide his fears to Minnie, and to daughter

Mary, who commuted to teach and who shared his concern. Merritt also served on the staff as farm manager, and Faith and her husband had joined the faculty and lived on campus.

Just as teenage years are difficult for parents to understand, so Elim's growing pains brought both joys and sorrows to its founder and its close friends. In such tempestuous seas, Carlton Spencer stood at Elim's helm, steering the ship according to those Other Hands placed upon his own. It was a lonely task, for he must make decisions that would be misunderstood by both newcomers and old-timers.

Ivan's counsel was sought and respected in meetings of the Board of Administration, but often he would withhold his opinion to talk privately with Carlton later. At such times, it was not certain as to who wore the mantle of leadership. Carlton's office light would burn into the wee hours of the morning as he sought answers from the Lord. Across the campus, another light would blink on and off—Ivan was not sleeping well.

In teaching his classes, Ivan sought earnestly to offset what seemed to him an academic imbalance, with a Spirit-led, revelatory approach to truth. The whole Word of God was within him a veritable treasure house, from which he brought forth truths new and old. Hungry-hearted students hung on his words, and often followed him about the campus in further conversation.

Ivan's method of teaching the Book of Revelation was unique. "Since the Spirit directed the writing of John's revelation," he would declare to his class, "then the best way to understand it is to wait upon the Lord together, for His Spirit to quicken its meaning to our hearts." He would then lead the class in a time of waiting and listening. Often prophetic utterances would come forth, perhaps even truly blessed illuminations of truth, but little of the letter of the Book of Revelation would be learned. Certainly one good came from this method—the avoidance of confusions that are usually engendered by the many conflicting interpretations of Revelations.

With most students, Ivan enjoyed a good rapport, even with those who contested his judgment on spiritual matters. And indeed, more than students began to question Ivan's judgment, as more and more sensational manifestations crept into the already sifted visitation movement—and Ivan enthusiastically endorsed them.

In an editorial, Ivan had declared, "In this present move of the Spirit, how easy it is to be occupied with *experiences*, *gifts*, *personalities*, and *revelations*, which in so many cases becloud our vision of Jesus. Surely the only way we can make spiritual progress in this hour of His moving is to see Jesus afresh. . . . As we become occupied with Him, we become occupied with the same thing which occupied Him. . . . The love of Christ still goes out to the lost world. . . . Away, all selfish interests, natural ambitions and borderland experiences. . . . Lord, in Thee alone shall the needs of this world be met!"

How God would test Ivan on these very words!

One test came in 1955.

Ivan's overriding quest for the supernatural made him easy prey for the trap of preoccupation with the increasing phenomena of "oil on the hands."* When Carlton and others of the school leadership refused to be endorsers of this supernatural sign, Ivan pressed for acceptance of the experience among friends and the students.

One day as Ivan spoke to his class regarding what God is doing today, he described the phenomenon of oil on the hands. One young student was not about to believe any such side issue of doctrine. He broke in with, "How can I know this is of God? You have taught us to apply four tests to any

---

*A phenomenon quite evident over a period of several years among healing evangelists wherein the palms of the evangelist would apparently exude oil as he laid his hands on the sick. This was experienced by Ivan Spencer at times.

teaching: Does it agree with, first, the Word? second, with my heart conviction? third, with the counsel of the brethren? and fourth, is it confirmed by circumstances? I can't see that this 'oil on the hands' passes any of these tests."

"And you never will see it, son," answered Ivan, in a tone that instantly rebuked him, "because you don't want to see it!"

Though an apology was soon offered, and lovingly accepted, the relationship could only continue on an "agree to disagree" basis. However, when a few years later the young man's name was up for consideration as an Elim missionary, and the board ruled his acceptance, it was Ivan who hurried out to find him. He embraced his former student as he told him the good news, and declared, "We want to send you, son," in sincere fatherly love. Today a man of stature in God, that missionary declares, "This showed me the bigness of the man, Ivan Spencer."

The particular prayer emphasis which began in the camp of 1954 continued during the school terms and in the conventions which followed. Outreach ministry from the school increased until there were twenty-five services each week being conducted by students. The Frodshams, Moores, and Ivan Spencers circulated among the churches and conventions, though Ivan more and more confined his visits to those accepting his message.

The 1955 Elim graduates included a European youth, Ernest Tanner, who was soon to become the founder of an extensive youth ministry in Germany and Switzerland; and a Cuban youth, Raul Trujillo, already active among Latin migrant workers of the Rochester area, and later a dynamic worker in Cuba's harvest.

To such as these, Ivan preached his baccalaureate message in the College Hall Chapel. Basing his remarks on the story of Jacob at Peniel, he urged, "Young people, if you have not had a time when God wrestled with you, I trust it will soon come, for when you are conquered by God you will come to know the meaning of the words, 'out of weakness made strong.' . . . Only God can make princes. . . . We can enter into sonship only as we take His life and nature—a new creation. . . . We will never know God in the depths of His nature except as we walk the path of suffering and separation."

Raul Trujillo would walk that path in Cuba's occupation by Castro and Communism.

Camp meetings at Elim were now witnessing the roots of the present charismatic renewal. Each summer, a growing number of denominational people hungry for God were in attendance. God did not disappoint them. Included among the leading speakers were David du Plessis, Paul Stutzman, Winston Nunes, and other men of apostolic stature. Always, too, there were the Elim missionaries who were home on furlough with exciting reports of revival to share, and fresh challenges of expansion.

During these crisis years, God spoke to Carlton to keep the priority on the sending forth of laborers into the harvest. Against great odds, Elim averaged sending out eight missionaries each year, and among them were some of the finest ever to serve on the fields.

Regarding his personal convictions, both for himself and the Elim fellowship, Carlton wrote the following, which reveals the extension of his personal vision beyond that previously projected by Ivan:

The question which confronts us personally is, "Have we dedicated our lives to the purposes of God for the Church and the world, in this climactic day?" . . . There is a charge from God laid upon us for these areas of the world. This is a definite part of the purpose for which God has apprehended us—a responsibility not only upon me, but upon the Elim fellowship.

At home, as in other parts of the world, a new
emphasis upon the work of the Holy Spirit, and the
accompanying empowering for deliverances, is being
seen in nearly every Christian fellowship. The rain of
the Spirit's outpouring is not confined to the ["latter
rain" and Pentecostal] groups who received so richly a
few years ago. What bearing does this have on us? It is
a call to an even clearer, broader vision of His purpose
to pour out His Spirit upon all flesh; and then to so
yield to Him in crucifixions of self and fresh infillings
of His Spirit, that we shall be enabled to move in any
and every channel He opens to us for witness or
ministry. . . . God save us from the concept of having
"arrived" in spiritual experience.

Carlton's expanding vision at this time was an attitude
basic to all of his future decisions and ministry, basic indeed
to Elim's present vision.

It is significant that guest speakers at Elim conventions
during these years included such men as J. Elwin Wright of
NAE; Robert Walker of *Christian Life*; Norman Grubb and
David Cornell of Worldwide Evangelization Crusade; C.M.
Ward of "Revivaltime"; Assemblies of God officials, Robert
Ashcroft and Philip Hogan; and Hubert Mitchell, then of
Youth for Christ. This growing involvement, including
non-Pentecostal fellowship, served to intensify the growing
division between Ivan and Elim's younger leadership.

However, that Ivan still retained his spiritual equilibrium
in heart conviction may be seen from some of his writing
during this period, amazingly practical stuff for this revival
mystic:

*Endtime Headaches.* . . . "Take heed . . . lest your

hearts be overcharged with surfeiting ('headaches'—Gr.)." . . . Could this not mean troubles, strains, worries, fears? Trying to keep up with the American way of life—the supply of all our wants instead of all our needs; the urge to possess by excessive labor, and by continuous payments carry a tremendous overload—resulting in these 'headaches'? How wonderful to be content with our present lot, settle back on the promises of God, have time to pray, read the Bible, and tend to our Gospel privileges. If we would listen and obey the checks of the Spirit we would find ourselves free for ministry to others. . . .

*Revival Suggestions for the Small Church.* . . . (1) Area fellowship meetings; (2) Special services by an anointed evangelist, periodically; (3) More conscientious work among the youth, with trained, spiritually, prepared workers; (4) Seek God for means of financing new projects for the church; (5) Attendance by the pastor at the Ministers' and Christian Workers' Seminar.

*Spiritual Decoys.* . . . John the Baptist pointed Jesus out to his disciples and said, "Behold the Lamb of God. . . . He must increase. . . . " By decoying men into our sect or point of view, and thus away from Jesus, we are apt to produce fanatics, instead of men and women of God. . . . John was a "friend of the Bridegroom"—he led his converts to Jesus. . . . If we remain a necessity to a new convert, we keep him from truly following Jesus. He becomes a disciple of a disciple. . . . The results are sectarianism, heresy, spiritual babyhood.

*Responsible Stewardship.* . . . Monies are being given carelessly to any appeal that comes by way of mail or over the radio. . . . Responsible stewardship is our duty. . . . Three tests should be applied to our giving: (1) Do we know the work to be genuine? (2) Does it really *need* our support? (3) Does it carry out the vision and burden upon our hearts?

In his visits among the pastors, Ivan often became deeply involved in doctrinal discussions. On one such visit, Minnie and Bernice were traveling with Ivan, sitting in the back seat while a young pastor held forth on some spiritual issue with Ivan up front. When they pulled into a filling station for gas, the ladies alighted to use the rest room. Later, with the gas tank filled, the attendant paid, and the discussion still going strong, Ivan pulled away from the station and was several miles down the road before he remembered his wife and daughter.

In December of 1955, Ivan and Minnie set out for Cuba, visiting Elim grads and churches on their way down to Miami. At each place they stopped, their "children" were delighted to have Dad and Mom Spencer as their guests. The delight was mutual. The Cardenas airport was a time of happy reunion with the Veaches, and the grandchildren.

Both the plane trip and being in Cuba were exciting firsts for Minnie, while Ivan was especially gratified to meet Raul Trujillo, now established in Cardenas, ready to become the pastor when the Veaches left for the States that month.

"Had a blessed time in meetings there," wrote Ivan, "and we laid the cornerstone for their new church."

For three weeks, Minnie and Ivan circulated about Cuba, holding meetings in the churches, often riding the jeep over red clay roads to villages where services were held outdoors, or under a brush arbor. The missionary wives were excited about entertaining Mom Spencer in their Cuban-style homes, with Cuban recipes; and the children amused her with their delightful Spanish-English chatter.

Ivan noted growth in all the churches he had previously visited. The daily radio programs were now reaching most of the Caribbean area and receiving amazing letters telling of miracles of healing and conversion. Ivan held a business meeting with the missionaries and Cuban pastors and workers, making wise decisions with their help for the future nationalizing of the work. Then, with the Veaches, Ivan and Minnie flew back to the States in time for Christmas, a tired but happy couple.

But as the winter wore on, tensions grew. Ivan's fears began to concentrate on persons, and frictions developed into factions, with Ivan standing at the point of divide. But God would not allow Ivan to "opt out" on his personal commitment to Christ because of his retirement, or his ripening age. The molding process God had begun in Ivan during RBTS days would continue faithfully to the end, His faithfulness revealed in chastisements as in blessings.

In November, Carlton headed for the mission field, "to gain a firsthand acquaintance with the needs of the field, so necessary to the developing missions program." Academic Dean, Chester Gretz, filled Carlton's position at Elim. And Milton Ennis, pastor from Mobile, Alabama, and member of Elim's Board of Trustees, accompanied Carlton to Africa. When their plane landed in Nairobi, Kenya, the two men hastened off to the challenges they knew awaited them.

# 17

*Ivan, A Revival Reminder For A New Generation*

Visitation was coming! Bud Sickler's face told the story when Carlton Spencer and Milton Ennis arrived dusty and tired after their long drive from Nairobi, through the big game country, to Mombasa. More exciting than their glimpses of herds of wild animals, clusters of thatch-roofed houses and people scarcely clad was this glowing surety of visitation from the throne of God. Bud exuded with faith that the T.L. Osborn Crusade scheduled to begin in a few weeks would bring the fullness of the awakening that had already begun.

The vision for visitation and a move of the Spirit actually had its beginning with the apostolic journeys of Ivan Spencer and Paul Stutzman, and a little later, Clair Hutchins and Joseph Mattsson-Boze. The latter had visited the work on the coast, had caught the challenge of God's heartthrob in the labors of the Sicklers, and had taken home a burden for this East African coastal city, long bound by heathendom, Mohammedanism, and Hinduism.

Those first few days in Mombasa, the workers met for prayer in the little Gospel Hall, joined often by the people of the church. There had been weeks and months of prayerful preparation, with the red-painted concrete floor wet with tears night after night as believers sought God for an awakening for their city. Carlton thrilled to hear their reports of assurances gained on their knees—of visions, also, which strengthened their faith for seeing God in action during the Crusade.

The remainder of the time preceding the Crusade was utilized in visiting upcountry areas, including two conventions. Not the least of Carlton's anticipations on this 600-mile trip to the interior was his reunion with his sister, Eva Butler, as well as the other Elim missionaries. When they arrived at Bukuria, preparations were underway for the Christmas convention soon to begin. Expectation ran high, and here, too, there had been that preparation of heart-searching and prayer so essential to a deep move of the Spirit.

What a glorious time it was—a veritable tidal wave of the Spirit. Carlton was privileged to behold the unusual sight of an African woman lost in worship and speaking in a language unknown to her—English! She sat with her babe at her breast, oblivious to all about her, even the babe's sucking and then slumber, as she worshiped on and on in English. Similar Baptisms swept through the crowds gathered, beyond numbering. God was also present to heal.

It was Carlton's privilege as well to assist Wallace Opunga, whom Ivan and Bud had previously ordained, in the baptizing of thirty-five converts in the river near their newest station at Suna. This event followed the dedication service of the new mission.

Then Carlton, Lindsay, and Ennis, with three African pastors, went on safari into Tanganyika to see officials about opening a mission, and to look over proposed mission sites. It was a great experience for Carlton, being so far away from all civilization. Carrying food and water, and all living supplies, through lion country; getting stuck in the mud and spending the night there; then going on to live among the people in primitive fashion; all served to awaken in him a feel for the missions responsibility he bore as Elim's leader.

Carlton left with a deepened burden for the need of the heathen. He wrote home, "There are so many areas in Kenya that yet are untouched by the full Gospel testimony. The other day Bud Sickler found representatives from large villages 200 miles away waiting for him in Mombasa. They had come to tell him of Pokomo tribespeople who had gathered and were going to 'stay until "Bwana Sickler" could come!' "

Returning to Mombasa to participate in the T.L. Osborn Crusade, Carlton found evidences of God's power everywhere. It was only the second day of the meetings, but already there was great excitement in the city. Bud and Fay Sickler were starry-eyed with wonder at the miracles. For so long, they had prayed and worked, and now in a matter of hours it was happening!

Carlton wrote home, "Osborn's preaching is simple, directed to heathen idol-worshipers and Moslems, but permeated with the Word. . . . The claims of Calvary are emphasized, and people testify to a change in heart and life. Heathen, Arabs, Goans, African Moslems, Whites, and Asian Indians all gather in one service—and meet God!"

He witnessed many marvels of healing, watching expressions of amazement turn to exuberant joy, and he knew God's awakening had come to East Africa. How his dad would love to be here, he thought. One thing sure, their missions outreach must accelerate immediately in order to conserve crusade results.

When the Osborns left, Bud continued in open-air teaching sessions where many who had been saved now received the Baptism in the Holy Spirit. Among these were young men—200 from that city alone—who became evangelists to their own people. It was plain that Elim must become more deeply involved in the preparation of workers—African as well as missionary—for harvest days.

Before leaving East Africa, Carlton made a stopover at Addis Ababa, Ethiopia, a visit pungent with memories of Hornell prayer meetings for the "three Abraham sisters" in their sojourn into this far country by faith. What a glorious outpouring of the Spirit they had witnessed before the interruption of their labors by the Italian occupation! Carlton shared in fellowship with the fruits of their labors, names familiar to him from the newsletters he had printed in the *Herald*. He left with the burden of challenge for a Holy Ghost visitation for the country of Ethiopia.

In Beirut, Lebanon, Carlton thrilled to see the tremendous growth of the school and mission founded by M.S. Shoucair. Included on staff were several Elim graduates. Again he sensed the air of urgency among the workers that he felt in Kenya. Retracing his father's footsteps, he flew to Switzerland. Here with John Owens at Chateau d'Oex, he ministered to his fine group of Bible school students.

It was the day before Missionary Convention, and up the hill and onto the campus drove Elim's beloved President, Elizabeth seated happily at his side. Carlton had been overseas for six months. The large porch that extended all across the front of the main building was full of Elim family members—including the school band—all waving, shouting, singing to greet him. And there was Chester Gretz—and mom and dad, bless 'em! Carlton stopped the car and climbed out rather shakily, moved by their song, "Great Is Thy Faithfulness." He tried to sing with them, but could only blink back the tears and praise the Lord.

After a general handshaking, and an embrace for his parents and fellow faculty members, Carlton was officially welcomed by a speech from the mightily relieved "ex-President pro tem," Chester Gretz. Carlton responded briefly—how could he possibly tell all he had experienced since he had last driven off campus? A whole new vista was opening before him—a fresh understanding of the words, "Ask of me, and I shall give thee the heathen." He got through to one student who wrote home, "He showed his deep concern and burden over the harvest fields he had just visited. . . . I am sure the benefit and blessing that will come to the school and the whole Elim fellowship through his new vision will more than repay the time, expense, and sacrifice involved in the trip."

Carlton was not home long before trouble erupted. Fc nearly two years, differences in emphasis, terminology, an opinion about what constituted the ministry of the Holy Spirit had been developing between Ivan and some newer members of the staff. Increasingly, the conflict was complicated by grave personality clashes.

"A whisperer separateth chief friends," and when Satan, who is master at the art, can find unwary channels, he will work his mischief to a frightening climax. God was testing Ivan on his own words, "How easy it is to be occupied with . . . personalities . . . which becloud our vision of Jesus." Ivan's fears, and now personal dislike, had precipitated the crisis. When school began that fall, the "academics vs. spirituals" controversy raged, with several joining Ivan in his crusade to save the classroom for the Spirit.

Soon the entire campus was immersed in the controversy. In such an atmosphere of strife, there could hardly be that spontaneous expression of the Holy Spirit that had characterized Elim's worship. The gentle Dove had withdrawn, "for where envying and strife is, there is confusion and every evil work."

Ivan was convinced that the matter must be dealt with and the leader dismissed from the staff. The directors called for a meeting with the staff member and several students who were spreading malicious gossip against him.

The confrontation was initially intense and painful, but the directors quickly detected that the student's accusations had no basis in fact. Discussion then shifted to Ivan's chief concern, the preservation of spontaneous ministry in the Spirit, and his doctrinal emphases on selectivity and restoration, all of which he felt were threatened by the other man's influence and counseling.

Backing Ivan in his convictions, one of the directors asked the faculty member, "Are you in full accord with the positions and goals of Elim's founder and directorate?"

"To the best of my understanding, I am," he answered, "though I cannot subscribe to placing priority on the extreme emphases of the doctrines of selectivity and restoration."

Painfully, Carlton chaired the meeting. He was heartsick when Ivan's fears influenced the final decision to ask the brother to resign his posts on the faculty and in the administration. Oh, the grief of a divided house! Carlton was caught between the factions, and his attempts to reconcile them only added fuel to the fire.

The schism was wide, but the passing years have a way of clarifying vision and restoring perspective, and God's healing is ever at work in the lives of those who are committed to Him. A few years later, the dismissed brother returned to campus, sought out Ivan, and each bared his heart to the other in true brotherly love, committing the past to God. Such miracles of healing seldom hit the headlines, but they as greatly magnify the grace of God as physical healings—perhaps more—and that is the purpose of Elim's story. So it was that the man who in his earliest acquaintance with Ivan had declared, "If I had a case to be judged, I would choose Ivan Spencer above all others to judge me," after such a difficult experience could exercise understanding of Ivan in his battle with fears, forgive him, and share in joyous fellowship again. How beautifully strong is this unity of the Spirit, for which Ivan all his life—except for this interval—paid dearly to gain, and maintain.

God's "fire of seven-fold heat" was surfacing Ivan's deep-seated problem with relinquishment, the surrendering of the work he had birthed into the Lord's hands. In giving up his leadership, Ivan saw the work going into younger hands that seemingly were not consumed by the same passions as he. Carlton suffered with his father, whose vision for Elim he shared; but also for the other younger brethren, whose vision he also understood and saw to be a furthering of Elim's training purposes.

With his fear of compromise still ruling him, Ivan's concern deepened into an insistence upon overemphases from which he had long been released. This reversion to teaching extreme doctrinal views belied his earlier admonition to "keep minor controversial doctrines in the background for the sake of unity." How far Ivan's fears had led him!

That spring, Carlton asked Elim's long time friend, Winston Nunes, to come to the school for teaching and for prayer. On their way home from Rochester, Winston asked serenely, "How are things going at the school, Carlton?" There was a sigh, and a bit of reluctant sharing; then a question.

"Is it possible to be just a Christian, and not become involved in such heartrending personality conflicts?"

Winston shot a look at his distressed brother, and thought of his own trying circumstances, and of his words of assurance from the Lord.

"Yes, if you can be satisfied with that. But all who are on the front lines of battle are sure to be under enemy fire!"

Arriving at the school, Winston and Carlton, with Elizabeth and several members of the faculty, closeted themselves for prayer. As the hours passed, several felt they had heard from the Lord. But Carlton found it difficult to see any answer—the situation seemed so desperate. Winston arose and left. Unknown to the others, he was hurrying across the campus to talk with Ivan.

"You are no longer able to provide leadership for the school yourself," Winston told him. "Your resistance to Carlton's leadership will only ruin all confidence in you, in him, and in Elim. You must stop contending and 'stand still and see the salvation of the Lord.' "

These words of wisdom became a wedge, inserted for the beginning of Ivan's release.

After further conversation, Winston returned to the prayer meeting.

That night in the service, Winston announced that Ivan Spencer "has something to say to us regarding his determination to no longer contend for controversial issues, but rather to stand by in prayer that God's will might be done." With his theme already developed for him, Ivan had only to acquiesce, which he did. Then Carlton was called to the altar for prayer. With others joining, Ivan was asked to pray for the school's president, his son. In those moments of prayer, the tide of antagonism began to turn. Victory after victory was to follow.

Bud Sickler returned from the African awakening that spring in time for the commencement convention. He addressed the graduating class with these words: "Get on your knees alone with God until a vision grips your soul that neither men nor demons can alter. . . . Give yourself to the vision of harvest and what God is doing. Refuse to be just another Bible school graduate going out to pastor a Pentecostal church with a circumscribed concept. Wherever God sends you, find out what God is doing in that place . . . be stirred!"

Ivan sat on the platform behind Bud, eyes misting with tears. Just twenty years ago, he had accepted the sixteen-year-old Bud into Elim. He would really have preferred to wait a year, but Bud was insistent and had scrupulously saved every dime he had earned that summer in order to come. Bud's earnest application to his studies and a missionary call, had often reminded Ivan of his own student days. He had freely deposited the seeds of his life and ministry into this young student's heart and mind, and now he was listening to the fruit of it. The vision he recognized as his own, but he noted wistfully the vibrant physical strength of this son in the Gospel. Oh, for youth again to match this ageless vision that threatened to consume him!

In the glow of his dawning release, Ivan, with Minnie, resumed his travels, his mellowing spirit becoming a greater blessing. When Eva returned on furlough from Africa, it was their joy to travel with her among the churches. Eva's missionary messages stirred even their own hearts to fresh vision, a marvelous antidote to Ivan's fears. How beautifully God provided for those sunset years of his life, granting a revitalizing force from the rising generation to whom he had given both physical and spiritual birth.

Ivan's release was Minnie's, for it had not been easy to stand with both Ivan and Carlton in their distress. Her intercessions for the situation had kept her vision clear, and she had often been able to counsel Carlton as a mother in Israel. Intercession—what better tool against confusion?— the getting of God's viewpoint in the matter.

During these years, Ivan's brother Vern came onto the scene again. Their father had passed away in his home, and when illness overtook him and his wife Flora, they were glad to accept Ivan's proffered hospitality for an extended visit. Vern's faithfulness at his home church deepened, and during chapel services at school, he would slip an offering into the plate, or give toward a missions need. When he and his wife passed away a few years later, his hoarded reserves were bequeathed in trust fund to Elim, equally for the school and missions, a clear affirmation of his change of heart!

Interim pastorates in Canada and the States began to open up to Ivan and Minnie. While in Lansing, Michigan, they had the pleasure of entertaining a guest speaker in their parsonage for a week—their daughter Eva. While still pastoring in Lansing, Ivan returned to Elim for an annual business meeting and resigned his administrative position as chairman of the ministers' fellowship.

The board issued a public statement "that we accept his resignation but here record that we recognize him as a spiritual father, leader, and apostle in the entire sphere of the functions and ministry of the Elim Missionary Assemblies." Carlton Spencer was named to the post vacated by his father, and remains today the revered Fellowship Chairman as well as President of the school, a revival leader in his own right.

It was at about that same time, in 1960, that a flamboyant new personality arrived on campus—the irrepressible Costa Deir. His initial stay with the faculty was brief, interrupted by five years in a pastorate, but, in 1965, he returned to serve as Elim's Missions Secretary, a post for which his Near Eastern origins and lovable ways have fitted him perfectly. He has served the Body of Christ broadly and deeply in that capacity, and is a constant inspiration to students through his classroom teaching.

Between pastorates, Ivan and Minnie lived in their little campus home, lovingly called "the Spencers' home." Minnie enjoyed the fellowship of the campus family, and Ivan busied himself with his fruit trees and garden—a farmer to the end. Many a cheering bouquet was left on an office desk, the receptionist's counter, or the kitchen table—with a smile and word of encouragement that matched them in cheer.

Though teaching less and less, due to his travels and failing health, Ivan retained personal rapport with the students. He would often leave his work of trimming campus lawns or shrubs to sit for a few minutes and chat with a student. It was said of him, "He has as much time for a freshman as for a visiting dignitary." His conversations with students would be studded with such terms as "purposes of God," "the dealings of God in your life," "your need for a vision."

The students learned the practicality of faith through examples he set them. One day, Ivan, with a group of students, planned to go get a load of apples for the school. When he arranged to drive the truck, the mechanic told him, "That old truck won't run. Even if you could get it started, it would quit again before you got back." The students heard Ivan's simple answer, "The Lord is a good mechanic." They piled into the truck, and it started like new. The 150-mile trip was made without a problem.

One student reported seeing Ivan lay his hand on a cow and pray God's blessing on her. It was customary for him to follow a planting time with prayer to God for a good harvest. His approach to God was a simple, common one which perhaps made him unique in our more sophisticated, materialistic day, but he would have been right at home with Francis of Assisi, or Madame Guyon, or the more modern mystic—a born-again "flower child." Perhaps this quality accounts for his appeal to the idealistic freshman student, with fire in his soul and stars in his eyes.

Ivan had infinite patience with such students, who would open up to him and discuss their problems at great length. But if he sensed insincerity, he was quick to strike at the root of their problem, his blunt honesty disarming them.

Camp meetings and conventions saw Ivan mixing among the crowds in delightful friendliness and hospitality, though now his friends and acquaintances were being outnumbered by new faces. One of these strangers, after Ivan had greeted him and gone on his way, asked, "Who's that old man who walks around here as if he owns the place?" The answer was simple, "He does! That's Ivan Spencer!"

Added to the faculty during these years were such men as Edwin Corley, Brian Bailey, Bernard (Bob) Mumford, and

David Edwards, encouraging Ivan to believe God for a bright Elim future. Though his fears did not completely disappear, they seemed to be subjected to the spirit of faith.

One last test came to Ivan when, over an issue of classroom procedures, a faculty member left, drawing a number of graduates and a few staff members with him in establishing another school along Spirit-ministry lines. Ivan's sympathies were sought, and long-subsided fears arose to plague him afresh. However, he turned to prayer, and peace returned. This further release of his own personal claim on the work he had birthed, opened his spirit to a renewing of vision.

There were social highlights for Ivan and Minnie during these years—a 50th Wedding Anniversary celebration in 1963 that drew many of their old friends from far places, as well as their complete family for a reunion—Eva coming from Africa, Ruth from Argentina, and Faith and Bernice from California. A 75th birthday Memorial Dinner was given in Ivan's honor at the school; then in 1968, an 80th birthday celebration, which again brought friends from great distances, and many heartwarming expressions of love.

Now restricted from travels by increasing weakness, Ivan was given a ministry of counseling in his home, as God sent ministers to him, to share problems and personal needs. One young minister was troubled by ecumenical discussions. Said Ivan, "We do not need union, but rather unity; there is union when two cats are tied together by the tail, but no unity!" To another young minister seeking advice for taking a new pastorate, he warned, "Remember, there will be no more fire in the pew than there is in the pulpit!"

Costa Deir, as Elim's Missions Secretary, never left the campus on an overseas trip without stopping in for "dad's" blessing in prayer.

"I'm leaving now, daddy," he would say, "and I want you to lay hands on me before I go. I know my going is really an extension of your vision." Costa today declares it an honor to perpetuate Ivan's ministry overseas.

Ivan had to be hospitalized when an injured thumb became infected, and needed amputation. Carlton was visiting him when Chester Gretz arrived—his wife was also undergoing surgery that hour. As in former years, the three became engrossed in conversation about the school and its objectives, the young people and their needs.

"They are so restless nowadays," Ivan observed with deep concern, "and I believe their restlessness is due to the fact that they have never known a real visitation of God. They must yet know one." Both younger men today vividly recall his words, especially challenging since they came from a mellowed spirit, and a concern that was above contention.

In 1967, Ivan rejoiced as much in the burning of the Lima mortgage as he had at Hornell in 1946. Excitement was growing in his spirit, for in the hours of quiet thought and prayer that were now his, faith was reaching out to make fresh claims for revival.

When God laid it upon the heart of a close friend of Elim to give a $100,000 inheritance to the school to be used as needed, Ivan declared that it should be used to build a tabernacle "to accommodate the people God has shown me will soon be streaming into Elim for the visitation that is coming."

Since one of the two new buildings recently added to the campus still remained to be paid for, the decision was not an easy one for Carlton. Such a building as was needed would require double that amount at the existing inflation prices and therefore still be equal to the original debt incurred when moving to Lima. Though those sixteen years had taught him many precious lessons in faith, he had only begun to enjoy the relief of lifted debt. Could he face such debt again, so quickly?

*Arise and build!* came God's word to him. With great

rejoicing, Elim was obedient, embarking on a building program that called for a $250,000 multi-purpose tabernacle, with dormitory and classrooms—nearly debt-free upon its dedication in 1972. It was Ivan's joy to be part of the groundbreaking service, turning the clods for his renewed vision. And it was Elim's joy to erect a sign on the building site that announced "Site of the new Ivan Q. Spencer Auditorium."

All during those months—years—of building, often in severest winter weather, Ivan would be on the site, joining the men in coffee-breaks, climbing about on the masonry to get close to the workmen and pass along his encouraging remarks. Often he would remind them of the word he had gotten from God—"Build it big—there is a great revival coming to Elim."

When his body was too weak for the walk across campus, Ivan would climb into his car at his door and drive around to the site. There he would watch from the car, calling the men over for a last-minute progress report—or for prayer. In fact, just one week before he died, he was standing out on the roof of the tabernacle, visiting with the men.

In one of his brief but spirited chapel talks to the students, he quoted, "My grace is sufficient for thee, for my strength is made perfect in weakness; most gladly therefore will I rather glory in mine infirmity that the power of Christ may rest upon me." He continued, "The testings of today have a purpose . . . preparation for last hour visitation. . . . My weakness is the most difficult lesson I've ever had to learn. With this weakness, comes a fresh need of consecration."

In another chapel talk, he compared the Latter Rain Revival with the present charismatic renewal. "Though much of the human element was in evidence in the latter rain movement, I believe that God intends the next visitation to be 100 percent pure, for He purposes to bring us to spiritual maturity. . . . We presently have a charismatic move of God with no outstanding leader and accompanied by supernatural movings . . . *but there is a spiritual preparation in progress* for more than the ministry we've known—*for a place in God—in union with Christ."*

Commencement of 1970 was held in the new tabernacle, though it was still unfinished. Ivan was present to join the rejoicing crowd that filled the auditorium, but he was too weak to participate in ministry. Wrapped in a shawl to protect him from drafts, he might have been a pathetic sight. But anyone noting his luminous smile and that gleam in his eye could not pity him. Camp meeting hosted an even larger attendance than commencement and found Ivan attending briefly each service as he was able. He gladly shared his vision of a coming visitation with any and all who would listen. It was always an appreciated word, coming from a revered father in the faith.

Secretly, deep in his heart, Ivan had held to the conviction that he would yet overcome physical death, living until the Lord's upward call would grant him power for translation with the "manchild company." Even in the face of encroaching weakness, and nights when breathing was difficult, he retained the hope, hoping against hope. Finally, he began to realize that he must go the way of all flesh. It seemed to him a bitter defeat, but actually the completeness of a truth—"O death where is thy sting; O grave where is thy victory?"—was about to break upon him; it was the completeness of the victory of Calvary that he had preached faithfully throughout his life.

As the valley of the shadow of death beckoned, Ivan resisted in brittle faith for translation. Peace fled as he tried to insist with God. The one day, he verbalized his heartbreaking disappointment to daughter Mary, who had stood for this teaching through the years. It was a tight moment for Mary, whose heart yearned to help her dad in his trial of faith, but God gave her the wisdom, and the power of conviction, needed. The words were practically the same as those Ivan himself had written for the *Herald* many years before when his dear friend Max Wood Moorhead had passed away:

"Dad, God is sovereign and can do as He pleases, and His choice is always best. Standing for the truth as you see it, is as acceptable to Him as the act of your translation. You have not failed God, but are rather like those faith worthies in Hebrews 11 who 'all died in faith, not having received the promises, but having seen them afar off, were persuaded of them, and embraced them.' You have 'kept the faith,' dad, and that's the important thing—for it is *faith* that pleases Him, you know." With that reminder, she concluded, and Ivan was content, blessedly content with the whole will of God.

On August 17, 1970, at the age of 81, Ivan passed into the presence of God, where revival is perpetual, and 100 percent pure! The Ivan Spencer Tabernacle was the scene of his triumphant coronation. Friends came from many states to pay tribute to the life and ministry of Ivan Spencer, a farm boy with a questing spirit, whose quest was now ended in triumph.

His good friend Paul Stutzman, a Bible school founder and principal in the Philippines, spoke at the funeral: "A mighty warrior has laid down his arms; a hero of faith is entering into his reward; a father in Israel is now being united with the family of God; a prince of the realm is receiving his inheritance; and a son of God is being welcomed home—Hallelujah!"

Just as mighty winds precede mighty rains, so Ivan Spencer, who lived ahead of his time, was a willow in the wind of spiritual awakenings that must precede the great endtime revival he envisioned. Though the horizon that beckoned proved to be beyond his reach, Ivan will not miss the fulfillment of his vision. From the ramparts of heaven, he will rejoice in the great ingathering soon to come—and as a willow by the watercourses, his roots will thirstily drink from that river which flows from the Throne of God—the source of all revival!

# EPILOGUE

## *Elim Today*

In practically every theater of world action, there may be found, perhaps submerged or under another label, influence which stems from a vision given to Ivan Spencer some fifty years ago.

As the willow's roots reach far beyond the spread of its branches, so Elim's influence extends far beyond its humble home base. Its unpretentious campus continually amazes those visitors from afar who judge its center by its circumference—perhaps through attendance among thousands at a west coast summer camp meeting, or by hearing of Elim from some renowned leader far removed from a humble Pentecostal heritage, such as Elim's.

But generally speaking, it is still a nonentity, much of its influence having lost the Elim label after leaving home base. And that is as it should be. Perhaps God needs just such catalysts as Elim—places where lives can undergo the Spirit's processing and yet remain free to operate in the direction in which God leads them.

What remains a wonder is that Elim survives to tell the story. Certainly no public relations program (for there is none) can assume the credit for a mushrooming student enrollment and missions outreach. Over and over, when tempted to "lean upon the arm of flesh," Elim has been encouraged to find that God Himself is managing its public relations. According to some amazing student testimonies, it was solely God's voice that directed them Elim-ward.

Howard was a high school honor graduate, pursuing agnostic and philosophic paths toward a dead end, when God apprehended his life. Through the Full Gospel Business Men's Fellowship, he was treated to an overseas airlift for missionary witness and returned primed for Gospel ministry. As he prayed regarding his next step, God plainly spoke a word foreign to him, "Elim." Some months later, through a brief encounter with an Elim student in another state, he learned that "Elim" was a Bible school located in upstate New York. He applied, was accepted, and is now a senior, active in outreach ministry.

Amalia was a young Christian in a Moslem country, suffering tortures both physically and emotionally at the hands of relatives. One day, in a daze of suffering, and having lost all hope of winning her family by remaining with them, she heard God's whispered direction in an unknown word, "Elim." Over succeeding months, it was a goal she constantly sought in all her hazardous travels from Egypt, to Lebanon, to the States. Arriving in New York City, she directed the cab driver, "To Elim, please." Noting his blank expression, she explained that a Christian in Lebanon had told her Elim was in New York. Still understandably confused, he took her to a missionary rest home, where a chance visitor "happened" to mention Elim in her hearing. Soon she was happily integrated with the Elim family in the study of God's Word.

Paul was one of the "flower children," disillusioned with the institutional church and yet seeking God with a passion. On a Los Angeles street corner, he was confronted with the

Gospel of salvation by grace, through faith, and within five minutes was saved and filled with the Spirit. Following the Lord's leading to enter the ministry, he attempted a seminary education, only to weary of study in all religions but the Gospel. Leaving, he joined a group with a deliverance and healing ministry. He had practically decided against further training when he heard from a concerned minister friend, "Paul, I've been praying for you and God tells me 'Elim.' " "What is that, and where?" Paul asked. The reply was vague, but the conviction remained that God had spoken. "Elim" came again through another minister, but this man, as the first, thought Elim to be somewhere in Canada, leaving Paul with no address to write for further information. Finally, he happened to enter a church service just in time to hear the pastor pray, "We thank You, Lord, for schools like Elim in Toronto. . . . " Further investigation revealed both Elim's identity and location, though the "Toronto" part of his prayer remains a mystery.

What Ivan could not have envisioned in his day was Elim's present ministry to a student body numbering hundreds, comprised not only of the usual Pentecostals and Spirit-filled denominationals, but of the "now" generation of flower children turned Jesus lovers; of the social drop-outs, the drug culture and cultist youths, now miraculously turned on for Christ; of the "anti-church" church young people, fuzzy idealists now in sharp focus with equal zeal for the Church universal; of the married couples successfully involved in community and business life, but who at God's call shrug it all off for the superior challenge of training for revival ministry.

Nor could Ivan have guessed the far-reaching impact of succeeding apostolic journeys by his successors in leadership, taking them on teaching seminars to nations he never saw. Perhaps this overseas extension of his vision is the most exciting of all. Let us start where we left off in the previous chapters, noting just those thrilling highlights of the vision's continuing fulfillment:

*East Africa*—The 1957 T.L. Osborn Crusade precipitated a flurry of training seminars for nationals, for the purpose of spreading the spiritual explosion effected by the Crusade. These were first held in Mombasa, then in other key cities; Nairobi, with missionary Paul Johansson as host, and Kampala, Uganda, with Arthur Dodzweit. American assistance in finances and teaching ministry came through Joseph Mattsson-Boze, Charles Weston, and others. Extension seminars fanned out through bush country where these hurriedly taught flaming national evangelists had multiplied themselves many times over. Accordingly, the number of bush churches zoomed from handfuls, to hundreds, to over 2000!

A stabilizing part of this expansion were the government schools, staffed with missionaries and national pastors who provided Bible classes and evangelistic influence, and also the growing training program among the women. Large evangelistic centers, each seating approximately a thousand, were built in the key cities to accommodate the burgeoning congregations. Branch churches and Sunday schools were established throughout each city. In 1967, Paul Johansson, with cooperation later from Cyril Cross and the British Assemblies of God, initiated a Bible school with a three-year training course, now graduating students of strong caliber for pastoral and other leadership positions. In Kampala, Arthur Dodzweit founded another such Bible school, assisted largely by David Clark, also an Elim graduate.

Elim missionaries in East Africa number thirty-five. Working closely with national organizations, including the PEFA (Pentecostal Evangelistic Fellowship of Africa), Elim's influence is strengthened by some 2000 national pastors and evangelists. Exciting breakthroughs continue, in spite of the many obstacles that always attend missionary endeavor.

*South America*—The Argentine Revival became continental in influence, with Sixto Lopez and his radio ministry a key in its spread throughout Colombia. To implement the uniting of the national revival movements, their leaders, with cooperation from Elim personnel, convened at strategic points for teaching, fellowship, and to seek God for further marching orders. The Peter Sedas, with Carlos and Celia (Brand) Estrada, are founders of a strong discipleship and church-planting program in Peru, with headquarters in Lima.

The more indigenous work in Argentina has been deeply influenced by George Veach, who continues to minister, with other Elim personnel, in conventions throughout South America. Strong and warm ties exist between many Argentine leaders and Elim, with Elim graduates being a vital part of continuing revival and "discipleship" ministry.

*Central America*—Elim grads and members of Elim's faculty at Lima, Kenneth and Helen Bennett could not be satisfied with the giving of their two sons to the cause of missions, nor with their own on-campus ministries and labors among the churches. Though in their fifties, they started life again in the rugged back country of Costa Rica. Here they founded the Elim Bible School of Guanacaste, and with a team of Elim grads and other missionaries and national workers, they reproduce revival ministers for their church-planting venture throughout the most backward villages of that nation.

*Europe*—Elim's influence has developed through Ernest Tanner's expanding Youth and Missions programs; through the ministries of Chester and Mary Ruth Gretz in Germany; through Elim graduates located in Scotland, England, and Spain; and through increasing cooperation with Youth With a Mission summer invasion teams, which each year include Elim students.

*Far East*—In addition to a continuing ministry in India, where Ivan visited, Elim personnel are increasingly involved in team ministry throughout the nations of Japan, Korea, Taiwan, Indonesia, the Philippines, New Zealand, and Australia. There are also several Elim-related Bible schools, with Elim graduates ministering on staff side by side with national workers and missionaries of other organizations. Specialized ministries include literature, orphanage, school, and youth evangelism work.

*Middle East*—Teaching seminars including Elim personnel are held in churches, schools, and organizations of all labels, in cooperation with an unprecedented move of the Spirit in that part of the world—this in addition to the fine missionary labors of Elim grads.

*United States*—As for Elim's expanding camp meeting ministry, Ivan saw only the beginnings of it on the west coast—in California, in cooperation with Ralph Mahoney and the World Missionary Assistance Plan which he founded. Since Ivan's death in 1970, other Elim-related summer camps or conferences have sprung up in Oregon and Washington; and in the east, in Virginia and Michigan. Similar thrusts extend into Mexico, in cooperation with Robert Blodget and other missionaries and national leaders.

Meanwhile, the home-based camp meeting, though not the largest, is steadily increasing. Its congregation from across the nation gives it a national influence, and it also has an enriching ministry for the whole area. For the past decade, Elim's camp meetings and conventions have played a vital role in the present "charismatic renewal" visitation. These meetings have implemented the spread of renewal by providing a neutral ground of common blessing and fellowship, supplying as well the deeply felt need for biblical teaching. Also involved in Elim's ministry to charismatics is its cooperation with the Full Gospel Business Men's Fellowship, the Christian Broadcasting Network, and various charismatic home, church, and college groups scattered throughout the northeast.

An inner-city ministry and training program, until recently carried out through the Elim City Training Center located in Brooklyn, New York, has absorbed a portion of Elim's personnel, finance, and prayers for the past ten years. Cooperation is now being given to similar training programs established by Elim grads and personnel: Pastor Robert Johansson and his church in Astoria, Long Island; Pastor Charles Vedral and his church in Manhattan; and Leslie and Dorothy Cole, formerly of Elim staff and missionaries to Ecuador, now engaged in a discipleship program among Spanish-speaking people, located in Elim's Brooklyn facilities. In addition, Elim cooperates with existing ministries to subculture needs throughout upstate New York.

Extension classes began as far back as the late fifties in New York City. Called BIONY, the Bible Institute of New York had a first year so successful that Elim assisted in opening three such schools the following year—in New York City, in New Jersey, and in Canada. It was a three-year course of night classes, creditable toward a full course of study at Elim's Lima campus. Though these particular night schools did not continue, Elim today cooperates with churches in Michigan and in upstate New York in conducting two night schools of formalized training, taught by Elim associates, and creditable toward Elim's three-year on-campus course of study. Plans are underway for more such teaching ministry to reach those who cannot become full-time day students. This will include an on-campus summer school program.

That Elim Bible Institute still retains its original objectives may be seen from a comparison of school catalog quotations gleaned from twenty-year intervals:

1934—"The aim of the Bible school is to give the student a working knowledge of the Bible, to prepare him for pastoral, evangelistic, missionary or other Christian ministry. A personal interest is taken in each student, to develop him in his prayer life, and in consistent Christian living."

1954—"The purpose is to train truly born-again, sober-minded young people for the work of the Lord. Because of the present rapid-moving revival, the need is urgent for ministers and workers with Spirit-given ministries. . . . This institute desires to foster and nourish the spiritual life of its students; to stimulate missionary and evangelistic zeal; and to serve as an instrument under God for His endtime purposes, 'that the man of God may be perfect, throughly furnished unto all good works.' "

1974—"In recognition of God's calling to involvement in His purposes throughout the earth, Elim Bible Institute continues in its commitment to: TEACH men and women the Word of God and, under the anointing of the Spirit, aid them in their personal discovery of truth; INSPIRE them to a vital relationship with Christ and His Body, the Church; PREPARE them to minister by the Spirit's enabling to the glory of God, to the needs of the Church, and to the world in which we live; and TRAIN them, through personal application of the truth, in discipleship—to become leaders among men through becoming followers of the Lord Jesus Christ."

God has always had special men of vision to provide leadership for the accomplishing of His will upon earth; but the undergirding of their work falls upon the "Aarons and Hurs" of each generation, who will labor, pray, counsel, finance, and otherwise sacrifice that God's ongoing purposes might be fulfilled in their day.

To such a Body ministry as this, Elim owes its existence. Each victory may be traced directly to the faithful stewardship of friends, faculty, and staff—men and women of God who over the years cast their lot with Elim, some for long periods of time, remaining faithful under extreme pressures. Salaries were never comparable to service rendered, but they looked upon their labors as an investment in the young lives they helped to train—and therefore a privilege, with eternal dividends involved.

The same might be said of the many donors who shared Elim's vision and sacrificed accordingly for the training of youth for endtime harvest.

We close this story with the consciousness that only as Elim continues to be small in its own eyes, decreasing that *He* might increase, will it proceed through these climactic days to the ultimate fulfillment of Ivan Spencer's vision of endtime revival ministry.

For a free copy of
**LOGOS JOURNAL**
*send your name and address to*
Logos Journal
Box 191
Plainfield, New Jersey 07060
*and say, "one free Journal, please."*